Praise for *Full Stack Serverless*

"Nader does a great job both making the case for serverless technologies and walking you through real-world scenarios. After reading this book and implementing the many sample projects, you will definitely have the skills you need to take advantage of serverless technologies and build better apps faster than ever."

—*Brice Wilson, Trainer and Consultant*

"Developing a full stack application doesn't have to be daunting. This book provides an easy, efficient, and effective way to get your application ready and available to your users."

—*Femi Oladeji, Frontend Developer, Temper*

"*Full Stack Serverless* will get you started with GraphQL, AppSync, and cloud development in no time, handling most of the complexity for you so you can focus on creating your app. Thumbs up!"

—*Oliver Kiessler, Full Stack Developer*

"Nader is bringing serverless web development to the masses. *Full Stack Serverless* is a can't-miss book for any web developer interested in using AWS Lambda, Cognito, and AppSync to improve their work."

—*Adam Rackis, Software Engineer, Riot Games*

Full Stack Serverless

Modern Application Development with React, AWS, and GraphQL

Nader Dabit

Beijing · Boston · Farnham · Sebastopol · Tokyo

Full Stack Serverless

by Nader Dabit

Published by O'Reilly Media, Inc., 1005 Gravenstein Highway North, Sebastopol, CA 95472.

O'Reilly books may be purchased for educational, business, or sales promotional use. Online editions are also available for most titles (*http://oreilly.com*). For more information, contact our corporate/institutional sales department: 800-998-9938 or *corporate@oreilly.com*.

Acquisitions Editor: Jennifer Pollock
Development Editor: Angela Rufino
Production Editor: Deborah Baker
Copyeditor: Piper Editing, LLC
Proofreader: Holly Bauer Forsyth

Indexer: Potomac Indexing, LLC
Interior Designer: David Futato
Cover Designer: Karen Montgomery
Illustrator: Rebecca Demarest

July 2020:   First Edition

Revision History for the First Edition
2020-07-13:   First Release
2020-07-31:   Second Release

See *http://oreilly.com/catalog/errata.csp?isbn=9781492059899* for release details.

978-1-492-05989-9

[LSI]

Table of Contents

Preface

Why I Wrote This Book

When I first learned how to code I had no idea how broad of a spectrum software development was. All I wanted to do was to build an app. Oh boy, I learned how naive I was at that time once I started digging into and piecing together all of the things that it took to accomplish what I wanted to do.

One of the main things I learned was that applications typically consisted of two main parts: frontend (or client-side code) and backend APIs and services. At the time, cloud technologies were in their infancy and learning how to build full stack applications was overwhelming to say the least! This was made even harder because I wanted to build native mobile apps, and I learned that building mobile apps was much tougher to get started with than building web applications.

Fast-forward almost 10 years and the landscape is starting to look much different. Things that once took a large team of developers to do can now sometimes be accomplished by a single developer. Tools like React Native, Flutter, and Cordova allow developers to build and ship cross-platform mobile applications using a single codebase. Cloud technologies like AWS Amplify, Firebase, and others allow the same developers to also leverage the cloud to build out the backends much more rapidly than ever before.

I think we are coming into a new paradigm where it is easier than ever to become a full stack developer and the definition of what a full stack developer *is* is starting to change. I wrote this book to lay out my vision of what this new paradigm looks like in practice and to showcase a technology that has been created specifically to take advantage of the most cutting-edge frontend and cloud technologies. What I am describing in this book is, in my opinion, the future of software engineering.

Who This Book Is For

This book is for any software engineer looking to build full stack applications, especially those interested in cloud computing. It is also aimed at frontend developers looking to learn how to use their existing skill set to build full stack applications using cloud technologies.

It is also a good resource for CTOs and startup founders looking to maximize efficiency and move with the most developer velocity possible while using the fewest resources. The techniques outlined in this book are ideal for rapid prototyping and fast experimentation, allowing developers and founders to get their idea to market quickly and have a product that is also scalable and durable should it succeed.

How This Book Is Organized

The goal of this book is to introduce you to all of the pieces needed to build a real-world and scalable full stack application using React and serverless technologies. It gradually introduces features (like authentication, APIs, and databases) and some techniques to implement these features, both on the frontend and backend, by building out different applications in each chapter.

Each application you create will build upon knowledge learned in the previous chapter. In the last chapter, you will build out a sophisticated application utilizing many of the cloud services needed to build real-world applications in your job or startup. When you have finished working through this book, you should have the knowledge and understanding needed to apply what you have learned to build serverless applications on your own using React and AWS cloud technologies.

Chapter 1, Full Stack Development in the Era of Serverless Computing
> In this chapter, I'll describe serverless philosophy, the characteristics and benefits of serverless applications, and introduce you to AWS and AWS Amplify CLI.

Chapter 2, Getting Started with AWS Amplify
> In this chapter, we will get going using AWS Amplify to create and deploy a serverless function. We'll create the function, then add the API and interact with it.

Chapter 3, Creating Your First App
> Here, we'll cover the basic process of creating a new full stack application from scratch by building a notes app. We will create a new React application, initialize a new Amplify project, add a GraphQL API, and then connect to and interact with the API from the client (React) application.

Chapter 4, Introduction to Authentication

In this chapter, we will walk through the process of adding authentication to an application. We will start by creating a new React application and adding basic authentication using the `withAuthenticator` higher-order component (HOC) from the AWS Amplify React library. We'll read the user's metadata and create a profile screen that will allow the user to see their information.

Chapter 5, Custom Authentication Strategies

In this chapter, we'll look closer at authentication by creating a custom authentication flow with React, React Router, and AWS Amplify. The app will have a sign-up screen, a sign-in screen, and a forgotten-password screen. Once logged in, there will be a main menu that will allow them to navigate to their profile page, a map page, and a welcome screen that will serve as the main view of the app.

Chapter 6, Serverless Functions In-Depth: Part 1 and Chapter 7, Serverless Functions In-Depth: Part 2

Here, we'll introduce serverless functions and how to interact with them in a React application. We'll walk through how to create, update, and delete serverless functions by creating an app that fetches shiba inu pictures from a CORS-protected API with our code living in an AWS Lambda function that we will create and configure using the AWS Amplify CLI.

Chapter 8, AWS AppSync In-Depth

In this chapter, we'll build upon what we learned in Chapter 3 by building a more complex API that includes many-to-many relationships and multiple authorization types. We'll build an event application that allows admins to create stages and performances. We'll enable all users to be able to read event information regardless whether they are signed in, but we'll only allow admin users who are signed in to create, update, or delete events and stages.

Chapter 9, Building Offline Apps with Amplify DataStore

In this chapter, we'll cover how to add offline functionality using Amplify DataStore.

Chapter 10, Working with Images and Storage

Here, we'll learn how to create a photo-sharing app that will allow users to upload and view images.

Chapter 11, Hosting: Deploying Your Application to the Amplify Console with CI and CD

In this final chapter, we'll take the photo-sharing app we created in Chapter 10 and deploy it to a live domain using the Amplify Console. We'll learn how to add continuous integration (CI) and continuous deployment (CD) by kicking off new builds when updates are merged to the master branch. Finally, we'll learn how to add a custom domain so your app will be live on a real URL that you own.

Conventions Used in This Book

The following typographical conventions are used in this book:

Italic
> Indicates new terms, URLs, email addresses, filenames, and file extensions.

`Constant width`
> Used for program listings, as well as within paragraphs to refer to program elements such as variable or function names, databases, data types, environment variables, statements, and keywords.

`Constant width bold`
> Shows commands or other text that should be typed literally by the user.

`Constant width italic`
> Shows text that should be replaced with user-supplied values or by values determined by context.

 This element signifies a tip or suggestion.

 This element signifies a general note.

Using Code Examples

Supplemental material (code examples, exercises, etc.) is available for download at *https://github.com/dabit3/full-stack-serverless-code*.

If you have a technical question or a problem using the code examples, please send email to *bookquestions@oreilly.com*.

This book is here to help you get your job done. In general, if example code is offered with this book, you may use it in your programs and documentation. You do not need to contact us for permission unless you're reproducing a significant portion of the code. For example, writing a program that uses several chunks of code from this book does not require permission. Selling or distributing examples from O'Reilly books does require permission. Answering a question by citing this book and quoting example code does not require permission. Incorporating a significant amount of example code from this book into your product's documentation does require permission.

We appreciate, but generally do not require, attribution. An attribution usually includes the title, author, publisher, and ISBN. For example: "*Full Stack Serverless* by Nader Dabit (O'Reilly). Copyright 2020 Nader Dabit, 978-1-492-05989-9."

If you feel your use of code examples falls outside fair use or the permission given above, feel free to contact us at *permissions@oreilly.com*.

O'Reilly Online Learning

 For more than 40 years, *O'Reilly Media* has provided technology and business training, knowledge, and insight to help companies succeed.

Our unique network of experts and innovators share their knowledge and expertise through books, articles, and our online learning platform. O'Reilly's online learning platform gives you on-demand access to live training courses, in-depth learning paths, interactive coding environments, and a vast collection of text and video from O'Reilly and 200+ other publishers. For more information, visit *http://oreilly.com*.

How to Contact Us

Please address comments and questions concerning this book to the publisher:

O'Reilly Media, Inc.
1005 Gravenstein Highway North
Sebastopol, CA 95472
800-998-9938 (in the United States or Canada)
707-829-0515 (international or local)
707-829-0104 (fax)

We have a web page for this book, where we list errata, examples, and any additional information. You can access this page at *https://oreil.ly/Full_Stack_Serverless*.

Email *bookquestions@oreilly.com* to comment or ask technical questions about this book.

For news and information about our books and courses, visit *http://oreilly.com*.

Find us on Facebook: *http://facebook.com/oreilly*

Follow us on Twitter: *http://twitter.com/oreillymedia*

Watch us on YouTube: *http://www.youtube.com/oreillymedia*

Acknowledgments

Thank you to my wife, Lilly, who has steadfastly supported me through my career and has gone above and beyond to keep our life in order as I worked late nights in the office and sometimes at home to write this book.

Thank you to my kids, Victor and Eli, who are awesome and my inspiration; I love you both very much. And thank you to my parents for putting me in a position to be able to learn things and get second, third, and fourth chances at life.

My thanks go to many groups and individuals: to the the entire AWS Mobile team who took a chance on hiring me fresh out of a tumultuous consulting career to join their team, and gave me the opportunity to work with the smartest people I've ever met. To Michael Paris, Mohit Srivastava, Dennis Hills, Adrian Hall, Richard Threlkald, Michael Labieniec, Rohan Deshpande, Amit Patel, and all of my other teammates who have showed me the ropes and helped me learn everything I needed to learn to get going at my new job. To Russ Davis, Lee Johnson, and SchoolStatus for giving the opportunity to learn bleeding-edge technology on the job that ultimately catapulted my career into consulting. To Brian Noah, Nate Lubeck, and my team at Egood, the first "real" tech job I had, for exposing me to the world of meetups and conferences as well as what it takes to be a great developer.

## CHAPTER 1

Full Stack Development in the Era of Serverless Computing

People have typically associated cloud computing with backend development and DevOps. However, over the past few years, this has started to change. With the rise of *functions as a service* (FaaS), combined with powerful abstractions in the form of managed services, cloud providers have lowered the barrier to entry for developers new to cloud computing, and for traditionally frontend developers.

Using modern tools, frameworks, and services like Amazon Web Services (AWS) Amplify and Firebase (among others), a single developer can leverage their existing skill set and knowledge of a single framework and ecosystem (like JavaScript) to build scalable full stack applications complete with all of the features that would in the past have required teams of highly skilled backend and DevOps engineers to build and maintain.

This book focuses on bridging the gap between frontend and backend development by taking advantage of this new generation of tools and services using the Amplify Framework. Here you'll learn how to build scalable applications in the cloud directly from your frontend environment using the Amplify Command Line Interface (CLI). You'll create and interact with various APIs and AWS services, such as authentication using Amazon Cognito, cloud storage using Amazon S3, APIs using Amazon API Gateway and AWS AppSync, and databases using Amazon DynamoDB.

By the final chapter, you will understand how to build real-world full stack applications in the cloud leveraging AWS services on the backend and React on the frontend. You'll also learn how to use modern APIs from React, like hooks, and functional components, as well as React Context for global state management.

Modern Serverless Philosophy

The term *serverless* is commonly associated with FaaS. Though you will find varying definitions as to what it means, the term has recently grown to encompass more of a philosophy than a shared definition.

Many times when people talk about serverless, they are really describing how to most efficiently deliver business value with a focus on writing business logic, instead of coding supporting infrastructure for your business logic. Adopting a serverless mindset allows you to do this by consciously going out of your way to find and leverage FaaS, managed services, and smart abstractions, while only building custom solutions if an existing service just doesn't yet exist.

More and more companies and developers are taking this approach, as it doesn't make sense to reinvent the wheel. With the increase in popularity of this philosophy, there has also been an explosion of services and tools made available from startups and cloud providers to provide offerings that simplify backend complexity.

For an academic take on what *serverless* means, you may wish to read the 2019 paper written by a group at UC Berkeley, "Cloud Programming Simplified: A Berkeley View on Serverless Computing,"[1]. In this paper, the authors expanded the definition of *serverless*:

> While cloud functions—packaged as FaaS (Function as a Service) offerings—represent the core of serverless computing, cloud platforms also provide specialized serverless frameworks that cater to specific application requirements as BaaS (Backend as a Service) offerings. Put simply, serverless computing = FaaS + BaaS.

Backend as a service (BaaS) typically refers to managed services like databases (Firestore, Amazon DynamoDB), authentication services (Auth0, Amazon Cognito), and artificial intelligence services (Amazon Rekognition, Amazon Comprehend), among other managed services. Berkeley's redefinition of what serverless means underscores what is happening in the broader spectrum of this discussion as cloud providers begin to build more and better-managed services and put them in this bucket of serverless.

Characteristics of a Serverless Application

Now that you understand something about the philosophy around serverless, what are some of the characteristics of a serverless application? Though you may get varying answers as to what serverless is, following are some traits and characteristics that are generally agreed upon by the industry.

---

1 Eric Jonas, Johann Schleier-Smith et al. "Cloud Programming Simplified: A Berkeley View on Serverless Computing" (Feb. 10, 2019), *http://www2.eecs.berkeley.edu/Pubs/TechRpts/2019/EECS-2019-3.html*.

Decreased operational responsibilities

Serverless architectures typically allow you to shift more of your operational responsibilities to a cloud provider or third party.

When you decide to implement FaaS, the only thing you should have to worry about is the code running in your function. All of the server patching, updating, maintaining, and upgrading is no longer your responsibility. This goes back to the core of what cloud computing, and by extension serverless, attempts to offer: a way to spend less time managing infrastructure and spend more time building features and delivering business value.

Heavy use of managed services

Managed services usually assume responsibility for providing a defined set of features. They are serverless in the sense that they scale seamlessly, don't require any server operations or need to manage uptime, and, most importantly, are essentially codeless.

Benefits of a Serverless Architecture

These days there are many ways to architect an application. The decisions that are made early on will impact not only the application life cycle, but also the development teams and ultimately the company or organization. In this book, I advocate for building your applications using serverless technologies and methodologies and lay out some ways in which you can do this. But what are the advantages of building your application like this, and why is serverless becoming so popular?

Scalability

One of the primary advantages of going serverless is out-of-the-box scalability. When building your application, you don't have to worry about what would happen if the application becomes wildly popular and you onboard a large number of new users quickly—the cloud provider will handle this for you.

The cloud provider automatically scales your application, running the code in response to each interaction. In a serverless function, your code runs in parallel and individually processes each trigger (in turn, scaling with the size of the workload).

Not having to worry about scaling your servers and databases is a great advantage. It's one less thing you have to worry about when architecting your application.

Cost

The pricing models of serverless architectures and traditional cloud-based or on-premises infrastructures differ greatly.

With the traditional approach, you often paid for computing resources whether or not they were utilized. This meant that if you wanted to make sure your application would scale, you needed to prepare for the largest workload you thought you might see regardless of whether you actually reached that point. This approach meant you were paying for unused resources for the majority of the life of your application.

With serverless technologies, you pay only for what you use. With FaaS, you're billed based on the number of requests for your functions, the time it takes for your function code to execute, and the reserved memory for each function. With managed services like Amazon Rekognition, you are only charged for the images processed and minutes of video processed, etc.—again paying only for what you use.

This allows you to build features and applications with essentially no up-front infrastructure costs. Only if your application begins seeing increasing adoption and scaling do you begin to have to pay for the service.

The bill from your cloud provider is only one part of the total cost of your cloud infrastructure—there's also the operations' salaries. That cost decreases if you have fewer ops resources.

In addition, building applications in this way usually facilitates a faster time to market, decreasing overall development time and, therefore, development costs.

Developer velocity

With fewer features to build, developer velocity increases. Being able to spin up the types of features that are typical for most applications (e.g., databases, authentication, storage, and APIs) allows you to quickly focus on writing the core functionality and business logic for the features that you want to deliver.

Experimentation

If you are not investing a lot of time building out repetitive features, you are able to experiment more easily and with less risk.

When shipping a new feature, you often assess the risk (time and money involved with building the feature) against the possible return on investment (ROI). As the risk involved in trying out new things decreases, you are free to test out ideas that in the past may not have seen the light of day.

A/B testing (also known as *bucket testing* or *split testing*) is a way to compare multiple versions of an application to determine which one performs best. Because of the increase in developer velocity, serverless applications usually enable you to A/B test different ideas much more quickly and easily.

Security and stability

Because the services that you are subscribing to are the core competency of the service provider maintaining them, you are usually getting something that is much more polished and more secure than you could have built yourself. Imagine that a company's core business model has been, for many years, the delivery of a pristine authentication service, having fixed issues and edge cases for thousands of companies and customers.

Now, imagine trying to replicate a service like that within your own team or organization. Though this is completely possible, choosing to use a service built and maintained by those whose only job is to build and maintain that exact thing is a safe bet that will ultimately save you time and money.

Another advantage of using these service providers is that they will strive for the least amount of downtime possible. This means that they are taking on the burden of not only building, deploying, and maintaining these services, but also doing everything they can to make sure that they are stable.

Less code

Most engineers will agree that, at the end of the day, code is a liability. What has value is the feature that the code delivers, not the code itself. When you find ways to deliver these features while simultaneously limiting the amount of code you need to maintain, and even doing away with the code completely, you are reducing overall complexity in your application.

With less complexity comes fewer bugs, easier onboarding for new engineers, and overall less cognitive load for those maintaining and adding new features. A developer can hook into these services and implement features with no knowledge of the actual backend implementation and with little to no backend code at all.

Different Implementations of Serverless

Let's take a look at the different ways that you can build serverless applications as well as some of the differences between them.

Serverless Framework

One of the first serverless implementations, the Serverless Framework, is the most popular. It is a free and open source framework, launched in October 2015 under the name JAWS, and written using Node.js. At first, the Serverless Framework only supported AWS, but then it added support for cloud providers like Google and Microsoft Azure, among others.

The Serverless Framework utilizes a combination of a configuration file (*serverless.yml*), CLI, and function code to provide a nice experience for people wanting to deploy serverless functions and other AWS services to the cloud from a local environment. Getting up and running with the Serverless Framework can present a somewhat steep learning curve, especially for developers new to cloud computing. There is much terminology to learn and a lot that goes into understanding how cloud services work in order to build anything more than just a "Hello World" application.

Overall, the Serverless Framework is a good option if you understand to some extent how cloud infrastructure works, and are looking for something that will work with other cloud providers in addition to AWS.

The AWS Serverless Application Model

The AWS Serverless Application Model (*https://oreil.ly/ApIoW*) (AWS SAM) is an open source framework, released November 18, 2016, and built and maintained by AWS and the community. This framework only supports AWS.

SAM allows you to build serverless applications by defining the API Gateway APIs, AWS Lambda functions, and Amazon DynamoDB tables needed by your serverless application in YAML files. It uses a combination of YAML configuration and function code and a CLI to create, manage, and deploy serverless applications.

One advantage of SAM is that it is an extension of AWS CloudFormation, which is very powerful and allows you to do almost anything in AWS. This can also be a disadvantage to developers new to cloud computing and not familiar with AWS services, permissions, roles, and terminology, as you have to already be familiar with how the services work, the naming conventions to set them up, and how to wire it all together.

SAM is a good choice if you are familiar with AWS and are only deploying your serverless applications to AWS.

Amplify Framework

The Amplify Framework is a combination of four things: CLI, client library, toolchain, and web-hosting platform. Amplify's purpose is to provide an easy way for developers to build and deploy full stack web and mobile applications that leverage the cloud. It enables not only features such as serverless functions and authentication, but also GraphQL APIs, machine learning (ML), storage, analytics, push notifications, and more.

Amplify provides an easy entry point into the cloud by doing away with terminology and acronyms that may be unfamiliar to newcomers to AWS and instead uses a category-name approach for referring to services. Rather than referring to the authentication service as Amazon Cognito, it's referred to as *auth*, and the framework just uses Amazon Cognito under the hood.

Other options

More companies have started providing abstractions over serverless functions, usually intending to improve the negative user experience traditionally associated with working directly with AWS Lambda. A few popular options among these are Apex, Vercel, Cloudflare Workers, and Netlify Functions.

Many of these tools and frameworks still actually use AWS or some other cloud provider under the hood, so you are essentially going to be paying more in exchange for what they argue is a better user experience. Most of these tools do not offer much of the other suite of services available from AWS or other cloud providers; things like authentication, AI and ML services, complex object storage, and analytics may or may not be part of their offerings.

If you are interested in learning other ways of developing serverless applications, I would recommend checking out these options.

Introduction to AWS

In this section, I'll give an overview of AWS and talk about why something like the Amplify Framework exists.

About AWS

AWS, a subsidiary of Amazon, was the first company to provide on-demand cloud computing platforms to developers. It first launched in 2004 with a single service: Amazon Simple Queue Service (Amazon SQS). In 2006, they officially relaunched with a total of three services: Amazon SQS, Amazon S3, and Amazon EC2. Since 2006, AWS has grown and remains the largest cloud computing provider in the world, continuing to add services every year. AWS now offers more than two hundred services.

With the current state of cloud computing moving more toward serverless technologies, the barrier to entry is being lowered. However, it is still often tough for either a frontend developer or someone new to cloud computing to get started.

With this new serverless paradigm, AWS saw an opportunity to create a framework that focused on enabling these traditionally frontend developers and developers new to cloud computing to get started building cloud applications.

Full Stack Serverless on AWS

Full stack serverless is about providing developers with everything needed on both ends of the stack to accomplish their objective of building scalable applications as quickly as possible. Here, we'll look at how you can build applications in this way using AWS tools and services.

Amplify CLI

If you're starting out with AWS, the sheer number of services can be overwhelming. In addition to the many services to sort between, each service often has its own steep learning curve. To help ease this, AWS has created the *Amplify CLI.*

The Amplify CLI provides an easy entry point for developers wanting to build applications on AWS. The CLI allows developers to create, configure, update, and delete cloud services directly from their frontend environment.

Instead of a service-name approach (as used by the AWS Console and many other tools, like CloudFormation), the CLI takes a category-name approach. AWS has many service names (for example, Amazon S3, Amazon Cognito, and Amazon Pinpoint), which can be confusing to new developers. Rather than using the service names to create and configure these services, the CLI uses names like *storage* (Amazon S3), *auth* (Amazon Cognito), and *analytics* (Amazon Pinpoint) to give you a way to understand what the service actually does versus simply giving the service name.

The CLI has a host of commands that allow you to create, update, configure, and remove services without having to leave your frontend environment. You can also spin up and deploy new environments using the CLI in order to test out new features without affecting the main environment.

Once you've created and deployed features using the CLI, you can then use the Amplify client libraries to begin interacting with the services from your client-side application.

Amplify client

Building full stack applications requires a combination of both client-side tooling and backend services. In the past, the main way to interact with AWS services was using an AWS software development kit (SDK) such as Java, .NET, Node.js, and Python. These SDKs work well, but none of them are particularly well-suited for client-side development. Before Amplify, there was no simple method for building client-side applications using AWS. If you look at the documentation for the AWS Node.js SDK, you'll also notice that it presents a steep learning curve for developers new to AWS.

The Amplify client is a library made especially to provide an easy-to-use API for JavaScript applications that need to interact with AWS services. Amplify also has client SDKs for React Native, native iOS, and native Android.

The approach that the Amplify client takes is to provide a higher level of abstraction and bake in best practices to provide a declarative, easy-to-use API. At the same time, it gives you full control over the interactions with your backend. It's also built especially with the client in mind, with features like WebSocket and GraphQL subscription support. It utilizes localStorage for the browser and AsyncStorage for React Native to store security tokens like `IdTokens` and `AccessTokens` to persist user authentication.

Amplify also provides UI components for popular frontend and mobile frameworks including React, React Native, Vue, Angular, Ionic, native Android, and native iOS. These framework-specific components allow you to quickly get up and running with common features like authentication and complex object storage and retrieval without having to build out the frontend UI and deal with state.

The Amplify Framework does not support the entire suite of AWS services; instead, it supports a subset of them with almost all of them falling into the category of serverless. Using Amplify, it wouldn't make much sense to offer support for interacting with with EC2, but it makes a lot of sense to offer support for working with Representational State Transfer (REST) and GraphQL APIs.

Amplify was created as an end-to-end solution to fill a previously unfilled gap, but it also encompasses a new way to build full stack cloud applications.

AWS AppSync

AWS AppSync is a managed *API layer* that uses GraphQL to make it easy for applications to interact with any data source, REST API, or microservice.

The API layer is one of the most important parts of an application. Modern applications typically interact with a large number of backend services and APIs; things like databases, managed services, third-party APIs, and storage solutions, among others. *Microservice architecture* is the usual term used for a large application built using a combination of modular components or services.

Most services and APIs will have varying implementation details, which creates a challenge when you're working with a microservice architecture. This leads to inconsistent and sometimes messy code, as well as more cognitive load on the frontend developers making requests to these APIs.

One good approach to working with a microservice architecture is to provide a consistent API gateway layer that then takes all of the requests and forwards them on to the backend services. This allows a consistent interaction layer for your client to interact with, making development easier on the frontend.

GraphQL, a technology created and open sourced by Facebook, offers an especially good abstraction for creating an API gateway. GraphQL introduces a defined and consistent specification for interacting with APIs in the form of three operations: *queries* (reads), *mutations* (writes/updates), and *subscriptions* (real-time data). These operations are defined as part of a main *schema* that also provides a contract between the client and the server in the form of GraphQL types. GraphQL operations are not bound to any specific data source, so you as a developer are free to use them to interact with anything from a database, an HTTP endpoint, a microservice, or even a serverless function.

Typically, when building a GraphQL API, you need to deal with building, deploying, maintaining, and configuring your own API. With AWS AppSync, you can instead offload the server and API management as well as the security to AWS.

Modern applications often also have concerns such as real-time and offline support. Another benefit of AppSync is that it has built-in support for offline (Amplify client SDKs) as well as real time (GraphQL subscriptions) to enable developers to build these types of applications.

In this book, you will be using AWS AppSync along with various data sources (like DynamoDB for NoSQL and AWS Lambda for serverless functions) as the main API layer.

Introduction to the AWS Amplify CLI

You will be using Amplify CLI throughout this book to create and manage your cloud services. To learn how it works, you'll be creating and deploying a service using the CLI in this section. Once the service is deployed, you'll also learn how to remove it and then delete any backend resources associated with the deployment. Let's take a look at how you can create your first service.

Installing and Configuring the Amplify CLI

To get started, you first need to install and configure the Amplify CLI:

```
~ npm install -g @aws-amplify/cli
```

 To use the CLI, you will first need to have Node.js version 10.x or greater and npm version 5.x or greater installed on your machine. To install Node.js, I recommend either visiting the Node.js installation page (*https://nodejs.org/en*) and following the installation instructions or using Node Version Manager (*https://github.com/nvm-sh/nvm*) (NVM).

After the CLI has been installed, you next need to configure it with an identity and access management (IAM) user in your AWS account. To do so, you'll configure the CLI with a reference to a set of user credentials (access key ID and secret access key). Using these credentials, you'll be able to create AWS services on behalf of this user directly from the CLI.

To create a new user and configure the CLI, you'll run the `configure` command:

```
~ amplify configure
```

This will walk you through the following steps:

1. *Specify the AWS region.*

   This will allow you to choose the region in which you'd like to create your user (and, by extension, the services associated with this user). Choose the region closest to you or a preferred region.

2. *Specify the username.*

   This name will be the local reference of the user that you will be creating in your AWS account. I suggest using a name that you'll be able to recognize later when referencing it, such as *amplify-cli-us-east-1-user* or *mycompany-cli-admin*.

Once you enter your name, the CLI will open up the AWS IAM dashboard. From here, you can accept the defaults by clicking Next: Permissions, Next: Tags, Next: Review, and Create user to create the IAM user.

In the next screen, you will be given the IAM user credentials: the access key ID and secret access key. See Figure 1-1.

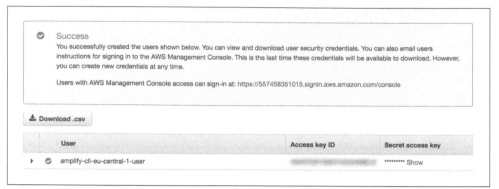

Figure 1-1. AWS IAM dashboard

Back in the CLI, paste in the values for the access key ID and secret access key. Now you've successfully configured the CLI and you can begin creating new services.

Initializing Your First Amplify Project

Now that the CLI has been installed and configured, you can create your first project. This step is usually done within the root of your client application. Since you will be using React for most of this book, we'll start by initializing a new React project:

```
~ npx create-react-app amplify-app

# after creating the React app, change into the new directory
~ cd amplify-app
```

Now you need to install the Amplify that you'll be using on the client. The libraries you'll be using are AWS Amplify and AWS Amplify React for the React-specific UI components:

```
~ npm install aws-amplify @aws-amplify/ui-react
```

Next, you can create an Amplify project. To do so, you'll run the `init` command:

```
~ amplify init
```

This will walk you through the following steps:

1. *Enter a name for the project.*

   This will be the local name for the project, usually something that describes what the project is or what it does.

2. *Enter a name for the environment.*

   This will be a reference to the initial environment that you will be working in. Typical environments in this workflow could be something like *dev*, *local*, or *prod* but could be anything that makes sense to you.

3. *Choose your default editor.*

   This will set your editor preference. The CLI will later use this preference to open your text editor with files that are part of the current project.

4. *Choose the type of app that you're building.*

   This will determine whether the CLI should configure, build, and run commands if you are using JavaScript. For this example, choose *javascript*.

5. *What JavaScript framework are you using?*

   This will determine a few base build and start commands. For this example, choose *react*.

6. *Choose your source directory path.*

   This allows you to set the directory where your source code will live. For this example, choose *src*.

7. *Choose your distribution directory path.*

   For web projects, this will be the folder containing the complied JavaScript source code as well as your favicon, HTML, and CSS files. For this example, choose *build*.

8. *Choose your build command.*

   This specifies the command for compiling and bundling your JavaScript code. For this example, use *npm run-script build*.

9. *Choose your start command.*

   This specifies the command to server your application locally. For this example, use *npm run-script start*.

10. *Do you want to use an AWS profile?*

    Here, choose *Y* and then pick the AWS profile you created when you ran `amplify configure`.

Now, the Amplify CLI will initialize your new Amplify project.

When the initialization is complete, you will have two additional resources created for you in your project: a file called *aws-exports* located in the *src* directory and a folder named *amplify* located in your root directory. These files contain the following:

The aws-exports file
> The *aws-exports* file is a key-value pairing of the resource categories created for you by the CLI along with their credentials.

The amplify folder
> This folder holds all of the code and configuration files for your Amplify project. In this folder you'll see two subfolders: the *backend* and *#current-cloud-backend* folders.

> *The backend folder*
>> This folder contains all of the local code for your project such as the GraphQL schema for an AppSync API, the source code for any serverless functions, and infrastructure as code representing the current local status of the Amplify project.

> *The #current-cloud-backend folders*
>> This folder holds the code and configurations that reflect what resources were deployed in the cloud with your last Amplify push command. It helps the CLI differentiate between the configuration of the resources already provisioned in the cloud and what is currently in your local *backend* directory (which reflects your local changes).

Now that you've initialized your project, you can add your first cloud service: *authentication*.

Creating and Deploying Your First Service

To create a new service, you can use the **add** command from Amplify:

```
~ amplify add auth
```

This will walk you through the following steps:

1. *Do you want to use the default authentication and security configuration?*

   This gives you the option of creating an authentication service using a default configuration (MFA on sign-up, password at sign-in), creating an authentication configuration with social providers, or creating a completely custom authentication configuration. For this example, choose *Default configuration*.

2. *How do you want users to be able to sign in?*

   This will allow you to specify the required sign-in property. For this example, accept the default by choosing *Username*.

3. *Do you want to configure advanced settings?*

This will allow you to walk through additional advanced settings for things like additional sign-up attributes and Lambda triggers. You do not need any of these for this example, so accept the default by choosing *No, I am done*.

Now, you've successfully configured the authentication service and are now ready to deploy. To deploy the authentication service, you can run the push command:

```
~ amplify push
```

4. *Are you sure you want to continue?*

Choose *Y*.

After the deployment is complete, your authentication service has successfully been created. Congratulations, you've deployed your first feature. Now, let's test it out.

There are several ways to interact with the authentication service in a React application. You can use the Auth class from Amplify, which has over 30 methods available (methods like signUp, signIn, signOut, etc.), or you can use the framework-specific components like withAuthenticator that will scaffold out an entire authentication flow, complete with preconfigured UI. Let's try out the withAuthenticator higher-order (HOC) component.

First, configure the React app to work with Amplify. To do so, open *src/index.js* and add the following code below the last import statement:

```
import Amplify from 'aws-amplify'
import config from './aws-exports'
Amplify.configure(config)
```

Now, the app has been configured and you can begin interacting with the authentication service. Next, open *src/App.js* and update the file with the following code:

```
import React from 'react'
import { withAuthenticator, AmplifySignOut } from '@aws-amplify/ui-react'

function App() {
  return (
    <div>
      <h1>Hello from AWS Amplify</h1>
      <AmplifySignOut />
    </div>
  )
}

export default withAuthenticator(App)
```

At this point, you can test it out by launching the app:

```
~ npm start
```

Now, your app should be launched with the preconfigured authentication flow in front of it. See Figure 1-2.

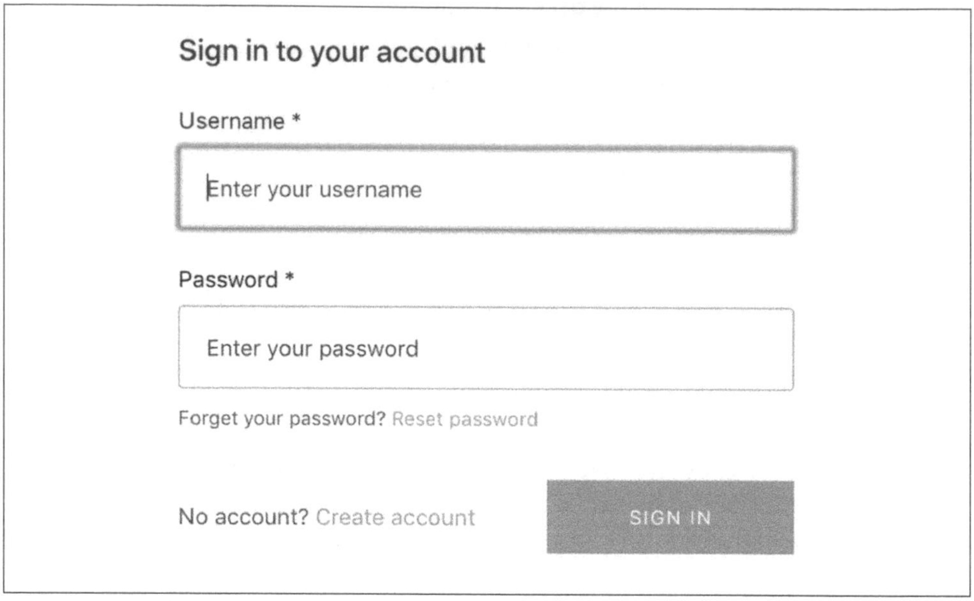

Figure 1-2. withAuthenticator HOC component

Deleting the Resources

Once you no longer need a feature or a project, you can remove it using the CLI.

To remove an individual feature, you can run the `remove` command:

```
~ amplify remove auth
```

To delete an entire Amplify project along with all of the corresponding resources that have been deployed in your account, you can run the `delete` command:

```
~ amplify delete
```

Summary

Cloud computing is growing at a rapid pace as more and more companies have come to rely on the cloud for the majority of their workloads. With this growth in usage, knowledge of cloud computing is becoming a valuable addition to your skill set.

The paradigm of serverless, a subset of cloud computing, is also rapidly growing in popularity among business users, as it offers all of the benefits of cloud computing while also featuring automatic scaling, while needing little to no maintenance.

Tools like the Amplify Framework are making it easier for developers of all backgrounds to get up and running with cloud as well as serverless computing. In the next chapters, you'll learn how to build real-world full stack serverless applications in the cloud, utilizing cloud services and the Amplify Framework.

## CHAPTER 2

Getting Started with AWS Amplify

At the core of most applications is the data/API layer. This layer could look like many things. In the serverless world, this usually will be composed of a combination of API endpoints and serverless functions. These serverless functions could be doing some logic and returning data, interacting with a database of some kind, or even interacting with another API endpoint.

There are two main ways of creating APIs with Amplify:

- A combination of Amazon API Gateway and a Lambda function
- A GraphQL API connected to some type of data source (database, Lambda function, or HTTP endpoint)

API Gateway is an AWS service that allows you to create API endpoints and route them to different services, often via a Lambda function. When you make an API call, it will route the request through API Gateway, invoke the function, and return the response. Using the Amplify CLI, you can create both the API Gateway endpoint as well as the Lambda function; the CLI will automatically configure the API to be able to invoke the Lambda function via an HTTP request.

Once your API is created, you then need a way to interact with it. Using the Amplify client you will be able to send requests to the endpoint using the Amplify API class. The API class allows you to interact with both GraphQL APIs as well as API Gateway endpoints, as shown in Figure 2-1.

In this chapter, you'll create your first full stack serverless app that will interact with a serverless function via an API Gateway endpoint. You'll use the CLI to create an API endpoint as well as a serverless function, and then use the Amplify client libraries to interact with the API.

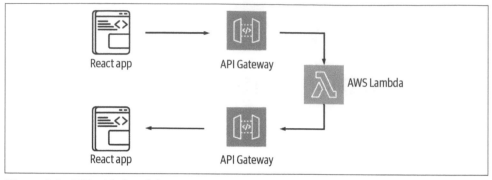

Figure 2-1. API with Lambda

At first, the app will fetch a hardcoded array of items from the function. You'll then learn how to update the function to make an asynchronous HTTP request to another API to retrieve data and return it to the client.

Creating and Deploying a Serverless Function

At the core of many serverless applications are *serverless functions*. Serverless functions run your code in *stateless compute containers* that are event-driven, short-lived (may last for one invocation), and fully managed by the cloud provider of your choice. These functions scale seamlessly and do not require any server operations.

While most people think of serverless functions as being invoked or triggered by an API call, these functions can also be triggered by a variety of different events. In addition to HTTP requests, a few popular ways to invoke a serverless function are via an image upload to a storage service, a database operation (like create, update, or delete), or even from another serverless function.

Serverless functions scale automatically, so there's no need to worry about your application if you get a large spike in traffic. The first time you invoke a function, the service provider will create an instance of the function and run its handler method to process the event. After the function finishes and returns a response, it will remain and process additional events if they come in. If another invocation happens while the first event is still processing, the service will then create another instance.

Serverless functions also have a payment model that is different from traditional infrastructure. With services like AWS Lambda, you only pay for what you use and are charged based on the number of requests for your functions and the time it takes for your code to execute. This is in contrast to provisioning and paying for infrastructure like servers regardless of whether they are being utilized.

Now that you know about serverless functions, let's take a look at how you can create a serverless function and hook it up to an API that will invoke it from an HTTP request.

Creating the React Application and Installing the Dependencies

To get started, you'll first need to create the React application. To do so, you can use npx:

```
~ npx create-react-app amplify-react-app
~ cd amplify-react-app
```

Next, you will need to install the dependencies. For this app, you'll only need the AWS Amplify library:

```
~ npm install aws-amplify
```

After installing the dependencies, you can now initialize a new Amplify project in the root of the React application:

```
~ amplify init

? Enter a name for the project: cryptoapp
? Enter a name for the environment: local
? Choose your default editor: <your-preferred-editor>
? Choose the type of app that you're building: javascript
? What javascript framework are you using: react
? Source Directory Path: src
? Distribution Directory Path: build
? Build Command: npm run-script build
? Start Command: npm run-script start
? Do you want to use an AWS profile? Here, choose *Y* and pick the AWS
  profile you created when you ran `amplify configure`.
```

Now, both the Amplify project and the React app have been successfully created and you can begin adding new features.

Creating a New Serverless Function with the Amplify CLI

In the next step, we'll create the serverless function that you will be using for this app. The app you are building in this chapter is a cryptocurrency app. At first, you will hardcode an array of cryptocurrency information in the function and return it to the client. Later in this chapter, you'll update this function to call another API (CoinLore) and asynchronously fetch and return data.

To create the function, run the following command:

```
~ amplify add function

? Select which capability you want to add: Lambda function
? Provide a friendly name for your resource to be used as a label for
```

```
       this category in the project: cryptofunction
  ? Provide the AWS Lambda function name: cryptofunction
  ? Choose the function runtime that you want to use: NodeJS
  ? Choose the function template that you want to use: Serverless express
    function (Integration with Amazon API Gateway)
  ? Do you want to access other resources created in this project from
    your Lambda function? No
  ? Do you want to invoke this function on a recurring schedule? No
  ? Do you want to configure Lambda layers for this function? No
  ? Do you want to edit the local Lambda function now? No
```

 If the function has successfully been created, you should see a message saying "Successfully added resource cryptofunction locally."

You should now see a new subfolder located within the *amplify* directory at *amplify/backend/function/cryptofunction*.

Walking Through the Code

When you created this resource, a new folder in *amplify/backend* was created named *function*. All of the functions created by the CLI will be stored in this folder. For now, you only have a single function, `cryptofunction`. In the *cryptofunction* folder, you will see a couple of configuration files as well as an *src* directory where the main function code is located.

Serverless functions are essentially just encapsulated applications running on their own. Because the function you created is in JavaScript, you'll see that there are all of the things you'd typically see in any JavaScript application, including *package.json* and *index.js* files.

Next, have a look at the function entry point located at *src/index.js*, in the *cryptofunction* folder. In this file you'll see that there is a function called `exports.handler`. This is the entry point for the function invocation. When the function is invoked, this is the code that is run.

You can handle the event directly in this function if you would like, but since you will be working with an API, a more useful way to do this is to proxy the path into an express app with routing (i.e., *http://yourapi/<somepath>*). Doing this gives you multiple routes in a single function as well as multiple HTTP request methods like `get`, `put`, `post`, and `delete` for each route. The *serverless express* framework provides an easy way to do this and has been built into the function boilerplate for you.

In *index.js*, you will see a line of code that looks like this:

```
awsServerlessExpress.proxy(server, event, context);
```

This code is where the event, context, and path are proxied to the express server running in *app.js*.

In *app.js*, you will then be able to create HTTP requests against whatever routes you create for your API (this example being a /coins route to fetch cryptocurrency).

Creating the /coins Route

Now that you have seen how the application is structured, let's create a new route in *app.js* and return some data from it. The route that you will be creating is a /coins route. This route will be returning an object containing a coins array.

Let's add the new route. Before the first app.get('/items') route, add the following code:

```
/* amplify/backend/function/cryptofunction/src/app.js /*

app.get('/coins', function(req, res) {
  const coins = [
    { name: 'Bitcoin', symbol: 'BTC', price_usd: "10000" },
    { name: 'Ethereum', symbol: 'ETH', price_usd: "400" },
    { name: 'Litecoin', symbol: 'LTC', price_usd: "150" }
  ]
  res.json({
    coins
  })
})
```

This new route has a hardcoded array of cryptocurrency information. When the function is invoked with this route, it will respond with an object containing a single property named coins that will contain the coins array.

Adding the API

Now that the function is created and configured, let's put an API in front of it so you can trigger it with an HTTP request.

To do this, you will be using Amazon API Gateway. API Gateway is a fully managed service that enables developers to create, publish, maintain, monitor, and secure REST and WebSocket APIs. API Gateway is one of the services supported by both the Amplify CLI as well as the Amplify client library.

In this section, you'll create a new API Gateway endpoint and configure it to invoke the Lambda function you created in the previous section.

Creating a New API

To create the API, you can use the Amplify add command. From the root of the project, run the following command in your terminal:

```
~ amplify add api

? Please select from one of the below mentioned services: REST
? Provide a friendly name for your resource to be used as a label for
  this category in the project: cryptoapi
? Provide a path: /coins
? Choose a Lambda source: Use a Lambda function already added in the
  current Amplify project
? Choose the Lambda function to invoke by this path: cryptofunction
? Restrict API access: N
? Do you want to add another path? N
```

Deploying the API and the Lambda Function

Now that the function and API have both been created, you need to deploy them to your account to make them live. To do so, you can run the Amplify push command:

```
~ amplify push

? Are you sure you want to continue? Y
```

Once the deployment has successfully completed, the services are live and ready to use.

You can use the Amplify CLI status command at any time to see the current status of your project. The status command will list out all of the currently configured services in your project and give you the status for each of them:

```
~ amplify status

Current Environment: local

| Category | Resource name  | Operation | Provider plugin   |
| -------- | -------------- | --------- | ----------------- |
| Function | cryptofunction | No Change | awscloudformation |
| Api      | cryptoapi      | No Change | awscloudformation |
```

The main thing to notice in this status output is the Operation. The Operation tells you what will happen the next time push is run in the project. The Operation property will be set to Create, Update, Delete, or No Change.

Interacting with the New API

Now that the resources have been deployed, you can begin interacting with the API from the React application.

Configuring the Client App to Work with Amplify

To use the Amplify client library in any application, there is a base configuration that needs to be set up, usually at the root level. When you create the resources, the CLI populates the *aws-exports.js* file with information about your resources. You will use this file to configure the client application to work with Amplify.

To configure the app, open *src/index.js* and add the following below the last import:

```
import Amplify from 'aws-amplify'
import config from './aws-exports'
Amplify.configure(config)
```

The Amplify Client API Category

After the client application has been configured, you can begin interacting with your resources.

The Amplify client library has various API categories that can be imported and used for various types of functionality, including `Auth` for authentication, `Storage` for storing items in S3, and `API` for interacting with REST and GraphQL APIs.

In this section, you will be working with the `API` category. `API` has various methods available—including `API.get`, `API.post`, `API.put`, and `API.del`—for interacting with REST APIs, and `API.graphql` for interacting with GraphQL APIs.

When working with a REST API, `API` takes in three arguments:

```
API.get(apiName: String, path: String, data?: Object)
```

apiName
    The name given when you create the API from the command line. In our example, this value would be `cryptoapi`.

path
    The path that you would like to interact with. In our example, we created `/coins`, so the path would be `/coins`.

data
    This is an optional object containing any properties you'd like to pass to the API, including headers, query string parameters, or a body.

In our example, the API call is going to look like this:

```
API.get('cryptoapi', '/coins')
```

The API returns a promise, meaning you can handle the call using either a promise or an `async` function:

```
// promise
API.get('cryptoapi', '/coins')
  .then(data => console.log(data))
  .catch(error => console.log(error))

// async await
const data = await API.get('cryptoapi', '/coins')
```

In the examples in this book, we'll be handling promises using `async` functions.

Calling the API and Rendering the Data in React

Next, let's call the API and render the data. Update *src/App.js* with the following:

```
// Import useState and useEffect hooks from React
import React, { useState, useEffect } from 'react'

// Import the API category from AWS Amplify
import { API } from 'aws-amplify'

import './App.css';

function App() {
  // Create coins variable and set to empty array
  const [coins, updateCoins] = useState([])

  // Define function to all API
  async function fetchCoins() {
    const data = await API.get('cryptoapi', '/coins')
    updateCoins(data.coins)
  }

  // Call fetchCoins function when component loads
  useEffect(() => {
    fetchCoins()
  }, [])

  return (
    <div className="App">
      {
        coins.map((coin, index) => (
          <div key={index}>
            <h2>{coin.name} - {coin.symbol}</h2>
            <h5>${coin.price_usd}</h5>
          </div>
        ))
```

```
      }
    </div>
  );
}
```

```
export default App
```

Then, run the app:

```
~ npm start
```

When the app loads, you should see a list of coins with their name, symbol, and price, as shown in Figure 2-2.

Figure 2-2. Fetching data from the API

Updating the Function to Call Another API

Next, you'll update the function to call another API, the CoinLore API, that will return dynamic data from the CoinLore service. The user will be able to add set filters like limit and start to limit the number of items coming back from the API.

To get started, you will first need a way to interact with an HTTP endpoint in the Lambda function. The library you will be using for this lesson is the Axios library. Axios is a promise-based HTTP client for the browser and Node.js.

Installing Axios

The first thing you need to do is install the Axios package in your function folder in order to send HTTP requests from the function. Navigate to *amplify/backend/function/cryptofunction/src*, install Axios, and then navigate back to the root of the app:

```
~ cd amplify/backend/function/cryptofunction/src
~ npm install axios
~ cd ../../../../../
```

Updating the Function

Next, update the /coins route in *amplify/backend/function/cryptofunction/src/app.js* with the following:

```
// Import axios
const axios = require('axios')

app.get('/coins', function(req, res) {
  // Define base url
  let apiUrl = `https://api.coinlore.com/api/tickers?start=0&limit=10`

  // Check if there are any query string parameters
  // If so, reset the base url to include them
  if (req.apiGateway && req.apiGateway.event.queryStringParameters) {
    const { start = 0, limit = 10 } = req.apiGateway.event.queryStringParameters
    apiUrl = `https://api.coinlore.com/api/tickers/?start=${start}&limit=${limit}`
  }

  // Call API and return response
  axios.get(apiUrl)
    .then(response => {
      res.json({ coins: response.data.data })
    })
    .catch(err => res.json({ error: err }))
})
```

In the preceding function, we've imported the Axios library and then used it to make an API call to the CoinLore API. In the API call, you can pass in a start and limit parameter to the request to define the number of coins to return, as well as to define the starting point.

In the req parameter, there is an apiGateway property that holds the event and the context variables. In the function just defined, there is a check to see if this event exists as well as the queryStringParameters property on the event. If the query StringParameters property exists, we use those values to update the base URL with the parameters. Using queryStringParameters, the user can specify the start and limit values when querying the CoinLore API.

Once the function is updated, you can deploy the updates by running the push command in your terminal:

```
~ amplify push

Current Environment: local

| Category | Resource name  | Operation | Provider plugin   |
| -------- | -------------- | --------- | ----------------- |
| Function | cryptofunction | Update    | awscloudformation |
| Api      | cryptoapi      | No Change | awscloudformation |
```

Updating the Client App

Now that you have updated the function, let's update the React app to give the user the option to specify the limit and start parameters.

To do so, you'll need to add fields for user input and give the user a button to trigger a new API request.

Update *src/App.js* with the following changes:

```
// Create additional state to hold user input for limit and start properties
const [input, updateInput] = useState({ limit: 5, start: 0 })

// Create a new function to allow users to update the input values
function updateInputValues(type, value) {
  updateInput({ ...input, [type]: value })
}

// Update fetchCoins function to use limit and start properties
async function fetchCoins() {
  const { limit, start } = input
  const data = await API.get('cryptoapi', `/coins?limit=${limit}&start=${start}`)
  updateCoins(data.coins)
}

// Add input fields to the UI for user input
<input
  onChange={e => updateInputValues('limit', e.target.value)}
  placeholder="limit"
/>
<input
  placeholder="start"
  onChange={e => updateInputValues('start', e.target.value)}
/>

// Add button to the UI to give user the option to call the API
<button onClick={fetchCoins}>Fetch Coins</button>
```

Next, run the app:

```
~ npm start
```

Summary

Congratulations, you've deployed your first serverless API!

Here are a few things to keep in mind from this chapter:

- Lambda functions can be triggered from a variety of events. In this chapter, we triggered the function using an API call from API Gateway.

- Lambda functions can be created from the Amplify CLI by using the command `amplify add function`, and APIs can be created using the command `amplify add api`.

- A single API Gateway endpoint can be configured to work with multiple Lambda functions. In the example in this chapter, we have only connected it to a single function.

- Lambda functions are essentially self-contained Node.js applications. In the example for this chapter, we chose to run an express application in order to handle REST methods like `get`, `post`, and `delete`, though we have only worked with a `get` call at this point.

- The `API` category from the Amplify client library can be used with both GraphQL as well as REST APIs.

## CHAPTER 3

Creating Your First App

In Chapter 2, you created a basic API layer using a combination of API Gateway and serverless functions. This combination is very powerful, but you have not yet interacted with a real database.

In this chapter, you will be creating a GraphQL API that interacts with a DynamoDB NoSQL database to perform CRUD+L (create, read, update, delete, and list) operations. You'll learn what GraphQL is, why developers are adopting it, and how it works.

We will be building a notes app that will allow users to create, update, and delete notes. It will also have GraphQL subscriptions enabled in order to see updates in real time. If another user is interacting with the app and they create a new note, our app will update with the new values in real time.

Introduction to GraphQL

GraphQL is an API implementation that is an alternative to REST. Let's have a look at what GraphQL is, what a GraphQL API consists of, and how GraphQL works.

What Is GraphQL?

GraphQL is an API specification. It is a query language for APIs and a runtime for fulfilling those queries with your data. It is, and can be used as, a replacement for REST and has some similarities to REST.

GraphQL was introduced by Facebook in 2015, though it had been used internally since 2012 (*https://oreil.ly/KtnOq*). GraphQL allows clients to define the structure of the data that is required from an API call so that they can know exactly what data structure is going to be returned from the server. Requesting data in this way enables a much more efficient way for client-side applications to interact with backend APIs and services, reducing the amount of under-fetching of data, preventing the over-fetching of data, and preventing type errors.

What Makes Up a GraphQL API?

A GraphQL API consists of three main parts: schema, resolvers, and data sources, as illustrated in Figure 3-1.

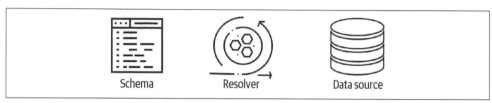

Figure 3-1. GraphQL API Design

The schema, written in GraphQL Schema Definition Language (SDL), defines the data model (types) and operations that can be executed against the API. The schema consists of base types (data models) and GraphQL operations like queries for fetching data; mutations for creating, updating, and deleting data; and subscriptions for subscribing to changes in data in real time.

Here is an example of a GraphQL schema:

```
# base type
type Todo {
  id: ID
  name: String
  completed: Boolean
}

# Query definitions
type Query {
  getTodo(id: ID): Todo
  listTodos: [Todo]
}

# Mutation definitions
type Mutation {
  createTodo(input: Todo): Todo
}

# Subscription definitions
type Subscription {
  onCreateTodo: Todo
}
```

Once the schema has been created, you can begin writing resolvers for the GraphQL operations defined in the schema (query, mutation, subscription). GraphQL resolvers tell the GraphQL operations what to do when being executed and will typically interact with some data source or another API, as shown in Figure 3-2.

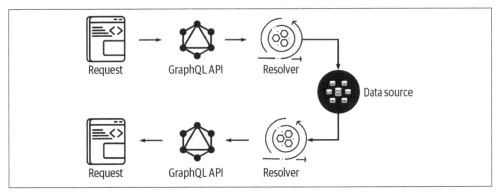

Figure 3-2. How GraphQL works

GraphQL Operations

GraphQL operations are how you interact with the API data sources. GraphQL operations can be similarly mapped to HTTP methods for RESTful APIs:

```
GET -> Query
PUT -> Mutation
POST -> Mutation
DELETE -> Mutation
PATCH -> Mutation
```

A GraphQL request operation looks similar to a JavaScript object with only the keys and no values. The keys and values are returned in the GraphQL operation response. Here's an example of a typical GraphQL query fetching an array of items:

```
query {
  listTodos {
    id
    name
    completed
  }
}
```

This request would return the following response:

```
{
  "data": {
    "listTodos": [
      { "id": "0", "name": "buy groceries", "completed": false },
      { "id": "1", "name": "exercise", "completed": true }
    ]
```

```
    }
  }
```

You can also pass arguments into a GraphQL operation. The following operation is a query for a Todo, passing in the ID of the Todo we'd like to fetch:

```
query {
  getTodo(id: "0") {
    name
    completed
  }
}
```

This request would return the following response:

```
{
  "data": {
    "getTodo": {
      "name": "buy groceries"
      "completed": false
    }
  }
}
```

Though there are many ways to implement a GraphQL server, in this book we will be using AWS AppSync. AppSync is a managed service that allows us to deploy a GraphQL API, resolvers, and data sources quickly and easily using the Amplify CLI.

Creating the GraphQL API

Now that you have a basic understanding of what GraphQL is, let's go ahead and start using it to build the Notes app.

The first thing you need to do is create a new React application and install the necessary dependencies. This app will be using the AWS Amplify library to interact with the API, uuid for creating unique ids, and the Ant Design library for styling:

```
~ npx create-react-app notesapp
~ cd notesapp
~ npm install aws-amplify antd uuid
```

Now, within the root of the new app, you can create the Amplify project:

```
~ amplify init

? Enter a name for the project: notesapp
? Enter a name for the environment: dev
? Choose your default editor: <your editor of choice>
? Choose the type of app that you're building: javascript
? What javascript framework are you using: react
? Source Directory Path: src
? Distribution Directory Path: build
```

```
? Build Command: npm run-script build
? Start Command: npm run-script start
? Do you want to use an AWS profile? Y
```

With the Amplify project initialized, we can then add the GraphQL API:

```
~ amplify add api

? Please select from one of the below mentioned services: GraphQL
? Provide API name: notesapi
? Choose the default authorization type for the API: API Key
? Enter a description for the API key: public (or some description)
? After how many days from now the API key should expire: 365 (or your
  preferred expiration)
? Do you want to configure advanced settings for the GraphQL API: N
? Do you have an annotated GraphQL schema? N
? Do you want a guided schema creation? Y
? What best describes your project: Single object with fields
? Do you want to edit the schema now? Y
```

Next, open the base GraphQL schema (generated by the CLI), located at *notesapp/ amplify/backend/api/notesapi/schema.graphql*, in your text editor. Update the schema to the following, and save it:

```
type Note @model {
  id: ID!
  clientId: ID
  name: String!
  description: String
  completed: Boolean
}
```

This schema has a main Note type containing five fields. A field can be either nullable (not required) or non-nullable (required). A non-nullable field is specified with a ! character.

The Note type in this schema is annotated with an @model directive. This directive is not part of the GraphQL SDL; instead, it is part of the AWS Amplify GraphQL Transform library.

The GraphQL Transform library allows you to annotate a GraphQL schema with different directives like @model, @connection, @auth, and others.

The @model directive we used in this schema will transform the base Note type into an expanded AWS AppSync GraphQL API complete with:

1. Additional schema definitions for queries and mutations (`Create`, `Read`, `Update`, `Delete`, and `List` operations)

2. Additional schema definitions for GraphQL subscriptions

3. DynamoDB database

4. Resolver code for all GraphQL operations mapped to DynamoDB database

To deploy the API, you can run the push command:

```
~ amplify push

? Are you sure you want to continue? Yes
? Do you want to generate code for your newly created GraphQL API: Yes
? Choose the code generation language target: javascript
? Enter the file name pattern of graphql queries, mutations and
  subscriptions: src/graphql/**/*.js
? Do you want to generate/update all possible GraphQL operations -
  queries, mutations and subscriptions: Y
? Enter maximum statement depth [increase from default if your schema is
  deeply nested]: 2
```

Once the deployment has completed, the API and database have successfully been created in your account. Next, let's open the newly created AppSync API in the AWS Console and test out a few GraphQL operations.

Viewing and Interacting with the GraphQL API

To open the API in the AWS Console at any time, you can use the following command:

```
- amplify console api

> Choose GraphQL
```

Once you've opened the AppSync console, click Queries in the lefthand menu to open the query editor. Here, you can test out GraphQL queries, mutations, and subscriptions using your API.

The first operation we'll try out is a mutation to create a new note. In the query editor, execute the following mutation (see Figure 3-3):

```
mutation createNote {
  createNote(input: {
    name: "Book flight"
    description: "Flying to Paris on June 1 returning June 10"
    completed: false
  }) {
    id name description completed
  }
}
```

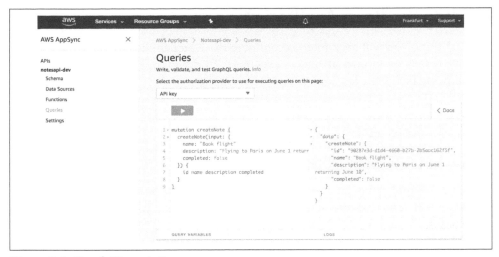

Figure 3-3. GraphQL mutation

Now that you've created an item, you can try querying for it. Let's try to query for all of the notes in the app:

```
query listNotes {
  listNotes {
    items {
      id
      name
      description
      completed
    }
  }
}
```

You can also try querying for a single note using the ID of one of the notes:

```
query getNote {
  getNote(id: "<NOTE_ID>") {
    id
    name
    description
    completed
  }
}
```

Now that we know the GraphQL API is deployed and functioning properly, let's start writing some frontend code.

Building the React Application

The first thing you will need to do is configure the React application to recognize the Amplify resources located at *src/aws-exports.js*. To do so, open *src/index.js* and add the following below the last import:

```
import Amplify from 'aws-amplify'
import config from './aws-exports'
Amplify.configure(config)
```

Listing Notes (GraphQL Query)

Now that the application has been configured, you can begin making calls against the GraphQL API. The first operation we will be implementing will be a query to list all of the notes.

The query will return an array and we will map over all of the items in the array, showing the note name, description, and whether or not it is completed.

In *src/App.js*, first import the following at the top of the file:

```
import React, {useEffect, useReducer} from 'react'
import { API } from 'aws-amplify'
import { List } from 'antd'
import 'antd/dist/antd.css'
import { listNotes } from './graphql/queries'
```

Let's take a look at some of the terms used in the preceding:

useEffect *and* useReducer
: React hooks

API
: This is the GraphQL client that we will be using to interact with the AppSync endpoint (similar to fetch or axios)

List
: UI component from the Ant Design library to render a list

listNotes
: The GraphQL query operation for fetching an array of notes

Next, we will need to create a variable to hold our initial application state. Because our application will be holding and working with multiple state variables, we will use the useReducer hook from React to manage state.

useReducer has the following API:

```
const [state, dispatch] = useReducer(reducer <function>, initialState <any>)
```

useReducer accepts a reducer function of type (state, action) => newState and initialState as arguments:

```
/* Example of some basic state */
const initialState = { notes: [] }

/* Example of a basic reducer */
function reducer(state, action) {
  switch(action.type) {
    case 'SET_NOTES':
      return { ...state, notes: action.notes }
    default:
      return state
  }
}

/* Implementing useReducer */
const [state, dispatch] = useReducer(reducer: <function>, initialState: <any>)

/* Sending an update to the reducer */
const notes = [{ name: 'Hello World' }]
dispatch({ type: 'SET_NOTES', notes: notes })

/* Using the state in your app */
{
  state.notes.map(note => <p>{note.name}</p>)
}
```

When invoked, the useReducer hook returns an array containing two items:

- The application state
- A dispatch function (this function allows you to update the application state)

The initial state of our Notes application will hold an array for the notes, form values, error, and loading state.

In *src/App.js*, add the following initialState object after the last import:

```
const initialState = {
  notes: [],
  loading: true,
  error: false,
  form: { name: '', description: '' }
}
```

Then create the reducer. For now, the reducer will only have cases to either set the notes array or set an error state:

```
function reducer(state, action) {
  switch(action.type) {
    case 'SET_NOTES':
      return { ...state, notes: action.notes, loading: false }
    case 'ERROR':
      return { ...state, loading: false, error: true }
    default:
      return state
  }
}
```

Next, update the main App function to create the state and dispatch variables by calling useReducer and passing in the reducer and initialState:

```
export default function App() {
  const [state, dispatch] = useReducer(reducer, initialState)
}
```

To fetch the notes, create a fetchNotes function (in the main App function) that will call the AppSync API and set the notes array once the API call is successful:

```
async function fetchNotes() {
  try {
    const notesData = await API.graphql({
      query: listNotes
    })
    dispatch({ type: 'SET_NOTES', notes: notesData.data.listNotes.items })
  } catch (err) {
    console.log('error: ', err)
    dispatch({ type: 'ERROR' })
  }
}
```

Now, invoke the fetchNotes function by implementing the useEffect hook (in the main App function):

```
useEffect(() => {
  fetchNotes()
}, [])
```

useEffect is similar to componentDidMount. useEffect will run after the initial render of the component is committed to the screen. The second argument to useEffect is an array of values, the effect of which depends on whether it is called again during a re-render. If the array is empty, it will not be called on additional renders. If the array contains values and those values change, the component will re-render.

The next thing you need to do is return the main UI for the component. In the main App function, add the following:

```
return (
  <div style={styles.container}>
    <List
      loading={state.loading}
      dataSource={state.notes}
      renderItem={renderItem}
    />
  </div>
)
```

Here we are using the List component from Ant Design. This component will map over an array (dataSource) and return an item for each item in the array by calling the renderItem function. Next, define renderItem (in the main App function):

```
function renderItem(item) {
  return (
    <List.Item style={styles.item}>
      <List.Item.Meta
        title={item.name}
        description={item.description}
      />
    </List.Item>
  )
}
```

Finally, create the styles for the components we will be using for this app:

```
const styles = {
  container: {padding: 20},
  input: {marginBottom: 10},
  item: { textAlign: 'left' },
  p: { color: '#1890ff' }
}
```

Now we are ready to run the app! In the terminal, run the start command:

```
~ npm start
```

When the app loads, you should see the current list of notes rendered to your screen, as illustrated in Figure 3-4.

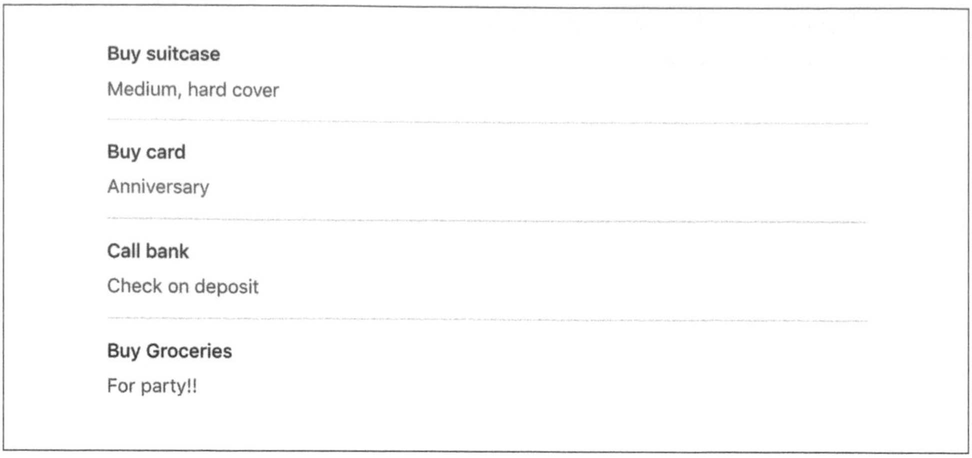

Buy suitcase

Medium, hard cover

Buy card

Anniversary

Call bank

Check on deposit

Buy Groceries

For party!!

Figure 3-4. Notes list

Creating Notes (GraphQL Mutation)

Now that you know how to query for a list of notes, let's take a look at how to *create* a new note. To do so, you'll need the following:

1. A form to create a new note

2. A function to update the state as the user types into the form

3. A function to add the new note to the UI and send an API call to create a new note

First, import the UUID library so you can create a unique identifier for the client. We do this now so that later on when we implement subscriptions we can identify the client that created the note. We will also import the Input and Button components from Ant Design:

```
import { v4 as uuid } from 'uuid'
import { List, Input, Button } from 'antd'
```

Next, you will need to import the `createNote` mutation definition:

```
import { createNote as CreateNote } from './graphql/mutations'
```

Then, create a new `CLIENT_ID` variable below the last import:

```
const CLIENT_ID = uuid()
```

Update the switch statement in the reducer to add three new cases. We will need a new case for the following three actions:

1. Adding a new note to the local state

2. Resetting the form state to clear out the form

3. Updating the form state when the user types

```
case 'ADD_NOTE':
  return { ...state, notes: [action.note, ...state.notes]}
case 'RESET_FORM':
  return { ...state, form: initialState.form }
case 'SET_INPUT':
  return { ...state, form: { ...state.form, [action.name]: action.value } }
```

Next, create the `createNote` function in the main App function:

```
async function createNote() {
  const { form } = state
  if (!form.name || !form.description) {
    return alert('please enter a name and description')
  }
  const note = { ...form, clientId: CLIENT_ID, completed: false, id: uuid() }
  dispatch({ type: 'ADD_NOTE', note })
  dispatch({ type: 'RESET_FORM' })
  try {
    await API.graphql({
      query: CreateNote,
      variables: { input: note }
    })
    console.log('successfully created note!')
  } catch (err) {
    console.log("error: ", err)
  }
}
```

In this function, we are updating the local state before the API call is successful. This is known as an *optimistic response*. It is done because we want the UI to be fast and to update as soon as the user adds a new note. If the API call fails, you can then implement some functionality in the catch block to notify the user of the error if you would like.

Now, create an `onChange` handler in the main App function to update the form state when the user interacts with an input:

```
function onChange(e) {
  dispatch({ type: 'SET_INPUT', name: e.target.name, value: e.target.value })
}
```

Finally, we will update the UI to add the form components. Before the List component, add the following two inputs and button:

```
<Input
  onChange={onChange}
  value={state.form.name}
  placeholder="Note Name"
  name='name'
  style={styles.input}
/>
<Input
  onChange={onChange}
  value={state.form.description}
  placeholder="Note description"
  name='description'
  style={styles.input}
/>
<Button
  onClick={createNote}
  type="primary"
>Create Note</Button>
```

Now, we should be able to create new notes using the form, as shown in Figure 3-5.

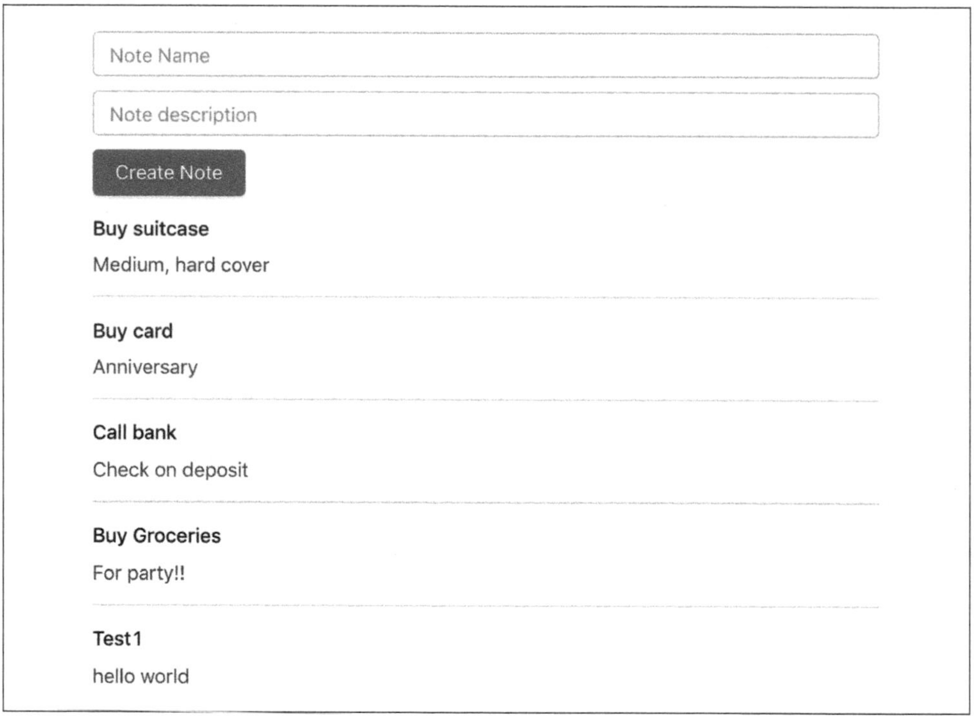

Figure 3-5. Creating a note

Deleting Notes (GraphQL Mutation)

Next, let's take a look at how to *delete* a note. To do so, we'll need the following:

1. A `deleteNote` function to delete the note both from the UI and from the GraphQL API

2. A button in each note to invoke the `deleteNote` function

First, import the `deleteNote` mutation:

```
import {
  createNote as CreateNote,
  deleteNote as DeleteNote
} from './graphql/mutations'
```

Then, create a `deleteNote` function in the main App function:

```
async function deleteNote({ id }) {
  const index = state.notes.findIndex(n => n.id === id)
  const notes = [
    ...state.notes.slice(0, index),
    ...state.notes.slice(index + 1)];
  dispatch({ type: 'SET_NOTES', notes })
  try {
    await API.graphql({
      query: DeleteNote,
      variables: { input: { id } }
    })
    console.log('successfully deleted note!')
    } catch (err) {
      console.log({ err })
  ]
}
```

In this function, we are finding the index of the note and creating a new notes array without the deleted note. We then dispatch the SET_NOTES action passing in the new notes array to update the local state and show an optimistic response. Next, we call the GraphQL API to delete the note in the AppSync API.

Now, update the `List.Item` component in the `renderItem` function to add a delete button to the `actions` prop that will call the `deleteNote` function, passing in the item:

```
<List.Item
  style={styles.item}
  actions={[
    <p style={styles.p} onClick={() => deleteNote(item)}>Delete</p>
  ]}
>
  <List.Item.Meta
   title={item.name}
```

```
    description={item.description}
  />
</List.Item>
```

Now, we should be able to delete notes (see Figure 3-6).

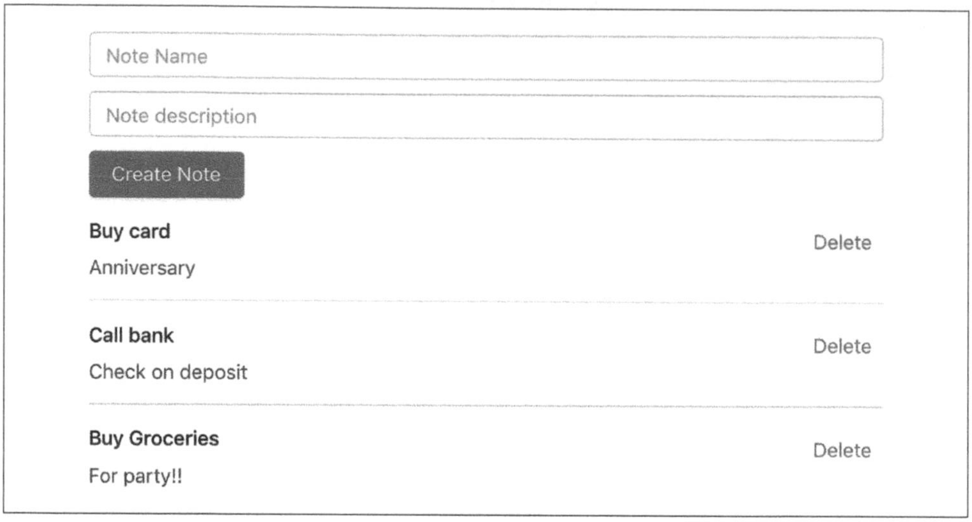

Figure 3-6. Deleting a note

Updating Notes (GraphQL Mutation)

The next piece of functionality we want to add is the ability to *update* a note to be completed. To do so, you'll need the following:

1. An updateNote function to update the note in the UI and in the GraphQL API

2. A button in each note to invoke the updateNote function

First, import the updateNote mutation:

```
import {
  updateNote as UpdateNote,
  createNote as CreateNote,
  deleteNote as DeleteNote
} from './graphql/mutations'
```

Next, create an updateNote function in the main App function:

```
async function updateNote(note) {
  const index = state.notes.findIndex(n => n.id === note.id)
  const notes = [...state.notes]
  notes[index].completed = !note.completed
  dispatch({ type: 'SET_NOTES', notes})
  try {
    await API.graphql({
      query: UpdateNote,
      variables: { input: { id: note.id, completed: notes[index].completed } }
    })
    console.log('note successfully updated!')
  } catch (err) {
    console.log('error: ', err)
  }
}
```

In this function, we are first finding the index of the selected note, then creating a copy of the notes array. We then update the completed value of the selected note to be the opposite of what it currently is. We then update the notes array with the new version of the note, set the notes array in the local state, and call the GraphQL API, passing in the note that needs to be updated in the API.

Finally, update the List.Item component to add an update button that will call the updateNote function, passing in the item. This component will render either comple ted or mark complete depending on the value of the completed Boolean of the item (based on whether completed is true or false):

```
<List.Item
  style={styles.item}
  actions={[
    <p style={styles.p} onClick={() => deleteNote(item)}>Delete</p>,
    <p style={styles.p} onClick={() => updateNote(item)}>
      {item.completed ? 'completed' : 'mark completed'}
    </p>
  ]}
>
```

Now, we should be able to update notes to be either *completed* or *not completed* (see Figure 3-7).

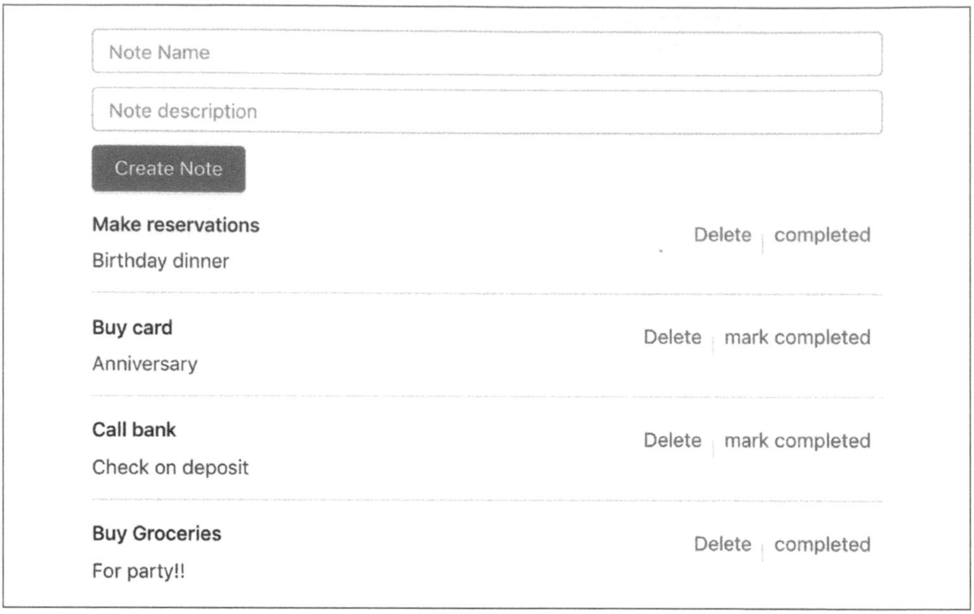

Figure 3-7. Updating a note

Real-Time Data (GraphQL Subscriptions)

The last piece of functionality we will implement is the ability to *subscribe to updates in real time*. The update that we'd like to subscribe to is when a new note has been added. When this happens, the functionality we'd like to implement is to have our application receive that new note, update the notes array with the new note, and render the updated notes array to our screen.

To do this, you will be implementing a GraphQL subscription. With GraphQL subscriptions, you can subscribe to different events. These events are usually some type of mutation (on create, on update, on delete). When one of these events happens, the data from the event gets sent to the client that initialized the subscription. It is then up to you to handle the data that comes in on the client.

To make this work, you'll only need to initialize the subscription in the `useEffect` hook and dispatch the `ADD_NOTE` type along with the note data when a subscription is fired.

First, import the `onCreateNote` subscription:

```
import { onCreateNote } from './graphql/subscriptions'
```

Next, update the `useEffect` hook with the following code:

```
useEffect(() => {
  fetchNotes()
  const subscription = API.graphql({
    query: onCreateNote
  })
    .subscribe({
      next: noteData => {
        const note = noteData.value.data.onCreateNote
        if (CLIENT_ID === note.clientId) return
        dispatch({ type: 'ADD_NOTE', note })
      }
    })
  return () => subscription.unsubscribe()
}, [])
```

In this subscription, we are subscribing to the `onCreateNote` event. When a new note is created, this event gets triggered and the `next` function is invoked, passing in the `note` data as the parameter.

We take the note data and check to see if our client is the application that created the note. If our client created the note, we return without going any further. If we are not the client that created the note, we dispatch the `ADD_NOTE` action, passing in the note data from the subscription.

Summary

Congratulations, you've deployed your first serverless GraphQL application!

Here are a few things to keep in mind from this chapter:

- The `useEffect` hook is similar to `componentDidMount` from the React lifecycle methods in that it runs after the component first renders.
- The `useReducer` hook allows you to manage application state and is preferable to `useState` when having more complex application logic.
- GraphQL *queries* are used for fetching data in a GraphQL API.
- GraphQL *mutations* are used for creating, updating, or deleting data in a GraphQL API.
- You can subscribe to API real-time events in a GraphQL API by using GraphQL *subscriptions*.

## CHAPTER 4

Introduction to Authentication

Authentication and *identity* are integral parts of almost any application. Knowing who the user is, what permissions they have, whether or not they are signed in, and having a unique identifier for the user allow your application to render the correct views and return the proper data for the currently signed-in user.

Most applications require mechanisms to handle user sign-up, user sign-in, password encryption, and updating, as well as countless other tasks around identity management. Modern applications often call for things like open authentication (OAUTH), multifactor authentication (MFA), and time-based on time passwords (TOTP).

In the past, developers had to hand roll all of this authentication functionality from scratch. This task alone could take a team of developers weeks, or even months, to get right and to do so securely. Today there are fully managed authentication services like Auth0, Okta, and Amazon Cognito that handle all of this for us.

In this chapter, you will learn how to properly and securely implement authentication in a React application using Amazon Cognito with AWS Amplify.

The app that you will be building is a basic application that requires authentication in order to be viewed and also has a profile page showing profile information about the signed-in user. If the user is signed in, they can navigate between a *public route*, a *profile route* with an authentication form, and a *protected route* viewable only to signed-in users.

If they are not signed in, they can only view the public route and authentication form on the profile route. If the user tries to access a protected route when they are not signed in, we want to redirect them to the authentication form so that they can sign in and then access the route once authenticated.

This app will also persist *user state*, so if they refresh the app or navigate away from it and come back, they will stay signed in.

Introduction to Amazon Cognito

Amazon Cognito is a fully managed *identity service* from AWS. Cognito allows for simple and secure user sign-up, sign-in, *access control*, and *user identity management*. Cognito scales to millions of users and also supports sign-in with social identity providers, such as Facebook, Google, and Amazon. It is also free for the first 50,000 users of any app.

How Amazon Cognito Works

Cognito has two main pieces: *user pools* and *identity pools*:

User pools
> These provide a secure user directory that stores all your users and scales to hundreds of millions of users. It is a fully managed service. As a serverless technology, user pools are easy to set up without having to worry about standing up any infrastructure. User pools are what manage all of the users that sign up and sign in to the account, and are what we will be focusing on in this chapter.

Identity pools
> These allow you to authorize users that are signed in to your application to access various other AWS services. Say you wanted to allow a user to have access to a Lambda function so that they could fetch data from another API; you could specify that while creating an identity pool. Where user pools come in is that the source of these identities could be a Cognito user pool or even Facebook or Google.

Cognito user pools allow your application to invoke various methods against the service to manage all aspects of user identity, including such items as:

- Signing up a user
- Signing in a user
- Signing out a user
- Changing a user's password
- Resetting a user's password
- Confirming an MFA code

Amazon Cognito Integration with AWS Amplify

AWS Amplify has support for Amazon Cognito in various ways. First of all, you can create and configure Amazon Cognito services directly from the Amplify CLI. Once you've created the authentication service via the CLI you can then call various methods (like `signUp`, `signIn`, and `signOut`) from your JavaScript application using the Amplify JavaScript client library.

Amplify also has preconfigured UI components that allow you to scaffold out entire authentication flows in just a couple of lines of code for frameworks like React, React Native, Vue, and Angular.

In this chapter, you'll be using a combination of the Amplify CLI, Amplify JavaScript client, and Amplify React UI components to build an application that demonstrates *routing*, *authentication*, and *protected routes*. You'll also use React Router for routing and Ant Design to give the application some basic styling (see Figure 4-1).

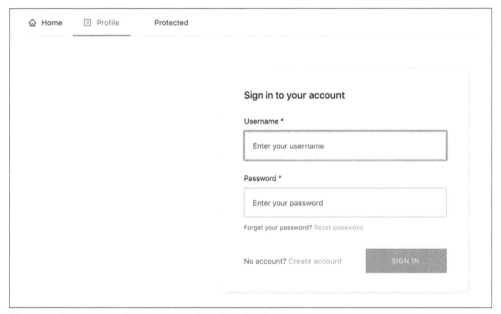

Figure 4-1. React with routing and authentication

Creating the React App and Adding Amplify

The first thing you'll do to get started is create the React application, install the necessary dependencies, and create the Amplify project.

To begin, open your terminal and create a new React application:

```
~ npx create-react-app basic-authentication
~ cd basic-authentication
```

Then install the AWS Amplify, AWS Amplify React, React Router, and Ant Design libraries:

```
~ npm install aws-amplify @aws-amplify/ui-react antd react-router-dom
```

Initialize a new Amplify project:

```
~ amplify init

# Follow the steps to give the project a name, environment name, and set
  the default text editor.
# Accept defaults for everything else and choose your AWS Profile.
```

With the Amplify project now initialized, we can create the authentication service. To do so, run the following command:

```
~ amplify add auth

? Do you want to use the default authentication and security
  configuration? Default configuration
? How do you want users to be able to sign in? Username
? Do you want to configure advanced settings? No, I am done.
```

Now the authentication service has been configured and you can deploy it using the `amplify push` command:

```
~ amplify push

? Are you sure you want to continue? Yes
```

The authentication service has been deployed, so let's start testing it out.

Client Authentication Overview

Using Amplify, there are two main ways to implement authentication on the client now that the service is up and running:

Auth *class*

The Amplify client library exposes an `Auth` class with over 30 different methods that allow you to handle everything associated with user management. Some examples of the methods available are `Auth.signUp`, `Auth.signIn`, and `Auth.signOut`.

Using this class, you can create a completely custom authentication flow based on your application's requirements. To do so, you have to manage all of the styling and application state yourself.

Framework-specific authentication components

The framework-specific libraries available in Amplify for frameworks like React, React Native, Vue, and Angular expose higher-level abstractions for managing authentication. These components will render an entire (customizable) authentication flow with only a few lines of code.

In Chapter 1, you had a chance to try out the higher-order component (HOC) from the AWS Amplify React library called withAuthenticator. Here, you'll be using this HOC along with routing to create protected routes and a profile view that can only be viewed if the user is signed in.

Building the App

The next step will be to go ahead and create the folder and file structure for the app.

Creating the File and Folder Structure

In your app, create the following files in the *src* directory:

```
Container.js
Nav.js
Profile.js
Protected.js
Public.js
Router.js
```

These files do the following:

Container.js

This file will hold a component you will be using to apply reusable styling to the other components.

Nav.js

In this component, you will create a navigation UI.

Profile.js

This component will render profile information about the logged-in user. This will also be the component where we add the authentication component for signing up and signing in.

Protected.js

This is the component we will be using as an example of how to create a protected route. If the user is signed in, they will be able to view this route. If they are not signed in, they will be redirected to the sign-in form.

Public.js

This is a basic route that will be viewable whether or not the user is signed in.

Router.js

This file will hold the router and some logic to determine the current route name.

Now that these files have been created, you have everything you need to begin writing some code.

Creating the First Component

To start, let's create the most simple component we will be using for the app—the `Container` component. This component is what we will be using to wrap all of our other components so that we can apply some reusable styles between the components:

```
/* src/Container.js */
import React from 'react'

const Container = ({ children }) => (
  <div style={styles.container}>
    { children }
  </div>
)

const styles = {
  container: {
    margin: '0 auto',
    padding: '50px 100px'
  }
}

export default Container
```

Using this component, you can now apply consistent styling across the entire app without having to rewrite your styles. You can then use it like this:

```
<Container>
  <h1>Hello World</h1>
</Container>
```

Anything that is a child of the `Container` component will be rendered with the styling set in the `Container` component. Doing this allows you to have a single place that you can control the styles. In case you want to make styling changes later, you only need to adjust one component.

Public Component

This component simply renders the name of the route to the UI and can be accessed whether or not the user is signed in. In this component, you will use the `Container` component to add some padding and margin:

```
/* src/Public.js */
import React from 'react'
import Container from './Container'

function Public() {
  return (
    <Container>
      <h1>Public route</h1>
    </Container>
  )
}

export default Public
```

Nav Component

The Nav (navigation) component will be utilizing the Ant Design library and React
Router. Ant Design will provide the Menu and Icon components to make a nice looking menu, and React Router will provide the Link component so that we can link and
navigate to different parts of the app.

You'll also notice that there is a current prop that is passed in to the component. This
prop represents the name of the current route. For this application the value will
either be home, profile, or protected. The current value is used in the selected
Keys array of the Menu component to highlight the current route in the navigation bar.
This value will be calculated in the Router component and passed into this component as a prop:

```
/* src/Nav.js */
import React from 'react'
import { Link } from 'react-router-dom'
import { Menu } from 'antd'
import { HomeOutlined, ProfileOutlined, FileProtectOutlined } from
        '@ant-design/icons'

const Nav = (props) => {
  const { current } = props
  return (
    <div>
      <Menu selectedKeys={[current]} mode="horizontal">
        <Menu.Item key='home'>
          <Link to={`/`}>
            <HomeOutlined />Home
          </Link>
        </Menu.Item>
        <Menu.Item key='profile'>
          <Link to='/profile'>
          <ProfileOutlined />Profile
          </Link>
        </Menu.Item>
```

```
      <Menu.Item key='protected'>
        <Link to='/protected'>
          <FileProtectOutlined />Protected
        </Link>
      </Menu.Item>
    </Menu>
  </div>
  )
}

export default Nav
```

Protected Component

The `Protected` component will be the protected, or private, route. If the user trying to access this route is signed in, they will be able to view this route. If they are not signed in, they will be redirected to the profile page to sign up or sign in.

In this component, you will be using the `useEffect` hook from React and the `Auth` class from AWS Amplify:

useEffect
> This is a React hook that allows you to perform side effects in function components. This hook accepts a function that is called when the function renders for the first time and, optionally, every additional time that it renders. By passing in an empty array as the second argument, we are choosing to only fire the function once: when the component loads. If you have used `componentDidMount` in a React class, `useEffect` has similar characteristics and use cases.

Auth
> This AWS Amplify class handles user identity management. You can use this class to do everything from signing a user up and signing them in to resetting their password. In this component we will be calling a method, `Auth.currentAu`
> `thenticatedUser`, that will check if the user is currently signed in and, if so, return data about the signed-in user:

```
/* src/Protected.js */
import React, { useEffect } from 'react';
import { Auth } from 'aws-amplify'
import Container from './Container'

function Protected(props) {
  useEffect(() => {
    Auth.currentAuthenticatedUser()
      .catch(() => {
        props.history.push('/profile')
      })
  }, [])
  return (
```

```
    <Container>
      <h1>Protected route</h1>
    </Container>
  );
}

export default Protected
```

When the component is rendered, we check to see if the user is signed in to the app by calling `Auth.currentAuthenticatedUser` in the `useEffect` hook. If this API call is not successful, that means the user is not signed in and we need to redirect them. We redirect them by calling `props.history.push('/profile')`.

If the user is signed in, then we take no action and allow them to view the route.

Router Component

The `Router` component will define the components and routes we want to have available in our application.

This component will also be setting the current route name that will be used in the `Nav` component to highlight the current route based on the `window.location.href` property.

The components that you will be using from React Router are `HashRouter`, `Switch`, and `Route`:

HashRouter

> This is a router that uses the hash portion of the URL (i.e., *window.location.hash*) to keep your UI in sync with the URL.

Switch

> `Switch` renders the first child route that matches the location. This is different than the default functionality of just using the router, which may render multiple routes that match the location.

Route

> This component allows you to define the component that you'd like to render based on a path parameter:

```
/* src/Router.js */
import React, { useState, useEffect } from 'react'
import { HashRouter, Switch, Route } from 'react-router-dom'

import Nav from './Nav'
import Public from './Public'
import Profile from './Profile'
import Protected from './Protected'
```

```
const Router = () => {
  const [current, setCurrent] = useState('home')
  useEffect(() => {
    setRoute()
    window.addEventListener('hashchange', setRoute)
    return () => window.removeEventListener('hashchange', setRoute)
  }, [])
  function setRoute() {
    const location = window.location.href.split('/')
    const pathname = location[location.length-1]
    setCurrent(pathname ? pathname : 'home')
  }
  return (
    <HashRouter>
      <Nav current={current} />
      <Switch>
        <Route exact path="/" component={Public}/>
        <Route exact path="/protected" component={Protected} />
        <Route exact path="/profile" component={Profile}/>
        <Route component={Public}/>
      </Switch>
    </HashRouter>
  )
}

export default Router
```

Inside the useEffect hook in this component, we set the route name by calling set
Route. We also set up an event listener to call setRoute whenever the route changes.

When declaring a Route component, you can pass in the component you would like
to render as the component prop.

Profile Component

The last component we need to finish our app is the Profile component. This component will do several things:

- Render the authentication form if the user is not signed in.
- Provide a sign-out button.
- Render the user's profile information to the UI.

Just like in Chapter 1, we are using the withAuthenticator HOC to render the
authentication flow by wrapping the Profile component in the default export. This
will show the sign-up/sign-in form if the user is not signed in, and if the user is
signed in will show the UI with the user's profile details.

To sign the user out, we use the AmplifySignOut UI component. This component will
sign the user out and re-render the UI to show the authentication form.

To display the user profile data, we use the `Auth.currentAuthenticatedUser` method. If the user is signed in, this method will return the user profile data along with information about the session. The information that we are interested in using for the profile are the username and user attributes, which include the phone number, email, and any other information gathered when the user signed up:

```
/* src/Profile.js */
import React, { useState, useEffect } from 'react'
import { Auth } from 'aws-amplify'
import { withAuthenticator, AmplifySignOut } from '@aws-amplify/ui-react'
import Container from './Container'

function Profile() {
  useEffect(() => {
    checkUser()
  }, [])
  const [user, setUser] = useState({})
  async function checkUser() {
    try {
      const data = await Auth.currentUserPoolUser()
      const userInfo = { username: data.username, ...data.attributes, }
      setUser(userInfo)
    } catch (err) { console.log('error: ', err) }
  }
  return (
    <Container>
      <h1>Profile</h1>
      <h2>Username: {user.username}</h2>
      <h3>Email: {user.email}</h3>
      <h4>Phone: {user.phone_number}</h4>
      <AmplifySignOut />
    </Container>
  );
}

export default withAuthenticator(Profile)
```

Styling the UI Components

Under the hood, the Amplify UI components are implemented using Web Components. This means we can target them as a first-class HTML element for CSS styling. We want our UI components to match the blue colors in the rest of our app. To do so, we can add the following CSS property to the bottom of *index.css* to define the colors we'd like to use:

```
/* src/index.css */

:root {
  --amplify-primary-color: #1890ff;
  --amplify-primary-tint: #1890ff;
```

```
    --amplify-primary-shade: #1890ff;
}
```

Configuring the App

Now the app is built. The last thing we need to do is update *index.js* to import the
Router and add the Amplify configuration. We also want to import the necessary CSS
for the Ant Design library:

```
/* src/index.js */
import React from 'react';
import ReactDOM from 'react-dom';
import './index.css';
import Router from './Router';
import 'antd/dist/antd.css';

import Amplify from 'aws-amplify'
import config from './aws-exports'
Amplify.configure(config)

ReactDOM.render(<Router />, document.getElementById('root'));
```

Testing the App

To test the app, we can now run the start command:

```
~ npm start
```

Summary

Congratulations, you've built out an authentication flow with routing and protected
routes!

Here are a few things to keep in mind from this chapter:

- Use the withAuthenticator HOC to quickly get up and running with a preconfigured authentication flow.

- Use the Auth class for more fine-grained control over authentication and to get
  data about the currently signed-in user.

- Ant Design helps you get started with preconfigured design without having to
  write any style-specific code.

## CHAPTER 5

Custom Authentication Strategies

In this chapter, we will be building and improving the app we completed in Chapter 4, where you learned how to use the `withAuthenticator` HOC to create a preconfigured authentication form. You also learned how to use React Router and the `Auth` class to create public and protected routes based on the user's signed-in state.

While this lays the foundation for what can be done with Amplify and the basics around authentication and routing, we want to go one step further and build a completely custom authentication flow so we know exactly what is going on under the hood and understand the logic and state needed to manage a *custom authentication form*. This means that we need to update our app to have custom forms for signing up, signing in, and resetting our password instead of using the `withAuthenticator` HOC.

We will also take the idea of *protected routes* one step further by creating a hook that we can reuse to wrap any component we are wanting to protect with authentication (instead of rewriting the logic in each component).

The `Auth` class, with over 30 different methods, is very powerful and allows you to handle all of the authentication logic that most applications demand. By the end of this chapter, you will understand how to use the `Auth` class and React state to build and manage a custom authentication form.

Creating the protectedRoute Hook

The first thing we will do is to create the custom `protectedRoute` hook that we will be using to protect any routes that require authentication. This hook will check for the signed-in user information, and if the user is not signed in, will redirect them to the sign-in page or another specified route. If the user is signed in, the hook will return and render the component passed in as an argument. By using this hook, we can do away with any duplicate logic around authentication that we may need across multiple components.

In the *src* directory, create a new file called *protectedRoute.js* and add the following code:

```
import React, { useEffect } from 'react'
import { Auth } from 'aws-amplify'

const protectedRoute = (Comp, route = '/profile') => (props) => {
  async function checkAuthState() {
    try {
      await Auth.currentAuthenticatedUser()
    } catch (err) {
      props.history.push(route)
    }
  }
  useEffect(() => {
    checkAuthState()
  }, [])
  return <Comp {...props} />
}

export default protectedRoute
```

This component uses the `useEffect` hook when the component loads to check if the user is signed in. If the user is signed in, nothing happens and the component that is passed in as an argument gets rendered. If the user is not signed in, we do a redirect.

The redirect route can either be passed in as the second argument to the hook, or if no redirect route is passed in, we set the default to be /profile. Now, we can use the hook to protect any component like this:

```
// Default redirect route
export default protectedRoute(App)

// Custom redirect route
export default protectedRoute(App, '/about-us')
```

Now that the protected route hook has been created, we can begin the refactor of our app. The next thing we may want to do is update the `Protected` component in our app to use this new `protectedRoute` hook. To do so, open *Protected.js* and update the component with this code:

```
import React from 'react';
import Container from './Container'
import protectedRoute from './protectedRoute'

function Protected() {
  return (
    <Container>
      <h1>Protected route</h1>
```

```
    </Container>
  );
}

export default protectedRoute(Protected)
```

Now this component is protected and users will continue to be redirected when trying to access it if they are not authenticated.

Creating the Form

The next thing we will want to do is create the main `Form` component. This component will hold all of the logic and UI for the following actions:

- Signing up
- Confirming sign up
- Signing in
- Resetting password

In Chapter 4, we used the `withAuthenticator` component that encapsulated most of this logic for us, but we will now be rewriting our own version of this from scratch. It is important to understand how to create and handle custom forms because you might work with custom designs and business logic that may not be compatible with abstractions like the `withAuthenticator` component.

The first thing we'll do is create the new component files that we will need. In the *src* directory, create the following files:

```
Button.js
Form.js
SignUp.js
ConfirmSignUp.js
SignIn.js
ForgotPassword.js
ForgotPasswordSubmit.js
```

Now that you have created these components, let's continue by creating a reusable button that will serve the submit button across all of the forms. In *Button.js*, add the following code:

```
import React from 'react'

export default function Button({ onClick, title }) {
  return (
    <button style={styles.button} onClick={onClick}>
      {title}
    </button>
  )
```

```
  }

const styles = {
  button: {
    backgroundColor: '#006bfc',
    color: 'white',
    width: 316,
    height: 45,
    fontWeight: '600',
    fontSize: 14,
    cursor: 'pointer',
    border:'none',
    outline: 'none',
    borderRadius: 3,
    marginTop: '25px',
    boxShadow: '0px 1px 3px rgba(0, 0, 0, .3)',
  },
}
```

The Button component is a basic component that accepts two props: title and onClick. The onClick handler will call the function associated with the button and the title component will render the text for the button.

Next, open *Form.js* and add the following code:

```
/* src/Form.js */
import React, { useState } from 'react'
import { Auth } from 'aws-amplify'
import SignIn from './SignIn'
import SignUp from './SignUp'
import ConfirmSignUp from './ConfirmSignUp'
import ForgotPassword from './ForgotPassword'
import ForgotPasswordSubmit from './ForgotPasswordSubmit'

const initialFormState = {
  username: '', password: '', email: '', confirmationCode: ''
}

function Form(props) {
  const [formType, updateFormType] = useState('signIn')
  const [formState, updateFormState] = useState(initialFormState)
  function renderForm() {}
  return (
    <div>
      {renderForm()}
    </div>
  )
}
```

Here, we've imported the individual form components (that we will be writing shortly) and created some initial *form state*. The items that we will be keeping up with in the form state are the input fields (`username`, `password`, `email`, and `confirmation Code`) for the authentication flow.

There's another piece of component state that keeps up with the type of form to be rendered: `formType`. Because the form components will be displayed all in one route, we will need to check what the current form state is and then render the Sign Up form, Sign In form, or Reset Password form.

`updateFormType` will be the function that switches between different form types. Once a user has successfully signed up, for example, we will call `updateForm Type('signIn')` to render the `SignIn` component so that they can then sign in.

The `renderForm` function will be updated later with some custom logic, but for now, does not do anything.

Next, add the following styles and default export to *Form.js*. The styles for some of the elements will be shared among the components, so we will be exporting the component as well as the styling:

```
const styles = {
  container: {
    display: 'flex',
    flexDirection: 'column',
    marginTop: 150,
    justifyContent: 'center',
    alignItems: 'center'
  },
  input: {
    height: 45,
    marginTop: 8,
    width: 300,
    maxWidth: 300,
    padding: '0px 8px',
    fontSize: 16,
    outline: 'none',
    border: 'none',
    borderBottom: '2px solid rgba(0, 0, 0, .3)'
  },
  toggleForm: {
    fontWeight: '600',
    padding: '0px 25px',
    marginTop: '15px',
    marginBottom: 0,
    textAlign: 'center',
    color: 'rgba(0, 0, 0, 0.6)'
  },
  resetPassword: {
    marginTop: '5px',
```

```
    },
    anchor: {
      color: '#006bfc',
      cursor: 'pointer'
    }
  }

export { styles, Form as default }
```

Next, let's go ahead and create the individual form components.

SignIn Component

The `SignIn` component will render the sign-in form. This component will accept two props, one for updating the form state (`updateFormState`) and one for calling the `signIn` function:

```
/* src/SignIn.js */
import React from 'react'
import Button from './Button'
import { styles } from './Form'

function SignIn({ signIn, updateFormState }) {
  return (
    <div style={styles.container}>
      <input
        name='username'
        onChange={e => {e.persist();updateFormState(e)}}
        style={styles.input}
        placeholder='username'
      />
      <input
        type='password'
        name='password'
        onChange={e => {e.persist();updateFormState(e)}}
        style={styles.input}
        placeholder='password'
      />
      <Button onClick={signIn} title="Sign In" />
    </div>
  )
}

export default SignIn
```

SignUp Component

The `SignUp` component will render the sign-up form. This component will accept two props, one for updating the form state (`updateFormState`) and one for calling the `signUp` function:

```
/* src/SignUp.js */
import React from 'react'
import Button from './Button'
import { styles } from './Form'

function SignUp({ updateFormState, signUp }) {
  return (
    <div style={styles.container}>
      <input
        name='username'
        onChange={e => {e.persist();updateFormState(e)}}
        style={styles.input}
        placeholder='username'
      />
      <input
        type='password'
        name='password'
        onChange={e => {e.persist();updateFormState(e)}}
        style={styles.input}
        placeholder='password'
      />
      <input
        name='email'
        onChange={e => {e.persist();updateFormState(e)}}
        style={styles.input}
        placeholder='email'
      />
      <Button onClick={signUp} title="Sign Up" />
    </div>
  )
}

export default SignUp
```

ConfirmSignUp Component

Once a user has signed up, they will receive a confirmation code for MFA. The `Con
firmSignUp` component holds the form that will handle and submit this MFA code.

This component will accept two props (in React, *props* means "properties," in regard
to passing data among components), one for updating the form state (`updateForm
State`) and one for calling the `confirmSignUp` function:

```
/* src/ConfirmSignUp.js */
import React from 'react'
import Button from './Button'
import { styles } from './Form'

function ConfirmSignUp(props) {
  return (
    <div style={styles.container}>
      <input
```

```
        name='confirmationCode'
        placeholder='Confirmation Code'
        onChange={e => {e.persist();props.updateFormState(e)}}
        style={styles.input}
      />
      <Button onClick={props.confirmSignUp} title="Confirm Sign Up" />
    </div>
  )
}

export default ConfirmSignUp
```

The next two forms will be for handling the resetting of a forgotten password. The first form (ForgotPassword) will take the user's username as an input and send them a confirmation code. They can then use that confirmation code along with a new password to reset the password in the second form (ForgotPasswordSubmit).

ForgotPassword Component

The ForgotPassword component will accept two props, one for updating the form state (updateFormState) and one for calling the forgotPassword function:

```
/* src/ForgotPassword.js */
import React from 'react'
import Button from './Button'
import { styles } from './Form'

function ForgotPassword(props) {
  return (
    <div style={styles.container}>
      <input
        name='username'
        placeholder='Username'
        onChange={e => {e.persist();props.updateFormState(e)}}
        style={styles.input}
      />
      <Button onClick={props.forgotPassword} title="Reset password" />
    </div>
  )
}

export default ForgotPassword
```

ForgotPasswordSubmit Component

The ForgotPasswordSubmit component will accept two props, one for updating the form state (updateFormState) and one for calling the forgotPassword function:

```
/* src/ForgotPasswordSubmit.js */
import React from 'react'
import Button from './Button'
```

```
import { styles } from './Form'

function ForgotPasswordSubmit(props) {
  return (
    <div style={styles.container}>
      <input
        name='confirmationCode'
        placeholder='Confirmation code'
        onChange={e => {e.persist();props.updateFormState(e)}}
        style={styles.input}
      />
      <input
        name='password'
        placeholder='New password'
        type='password'
        onChange={e => {e.persist();props.updateFormState(e)}}
        style={styles.input}
      />
      <Button onClick={props.forgotPasswordSubmit} title="Save new password" />
    </div>
  )
}

export default ForgotPasswordSubmit
```

Completing Form.js

Now that all of the individual form components have been created, we can update *Form.js* to use these new components.

The next thing we will do is open *Form.js* and create the functions that will interact with the authentication service. These functions—signIn, signUp, confirmSignUp, forgotPassword, and forgotPasswordSubmit—will be passed as props to the individual form components.

Below the last import, add the following code:

```
/* src/Form.js */
async function signIn({ username, password }, setUser) {
  try {
    const user = await Auth.signIn(username, password)
    const userInfo = { username: user.username, ...user.attributes }
    setUser(userInfo)
  } catch (err) {
    console.log('error signing up..', err)
  }
}

async function signUp({ username, password, email }, updateFormType) {
  try {
    await Auth.signUp({
      username, password, attributes: { email }
```

```
    })
    console.log('sign up success!')
    updateFormType('confirmSignUp')
  } catch (err) {
    console.log('error signing up..', err)
  }
}

async function confirmSignUp({ username, confirmationCode }, updateFormType) {
  try {
    await Auth.confirmSignUp(username, confirmationCode)
    updateFormType('signIn')
  } catch (err) {
    console.log('error signing up..', err)
  }
}

async function forgotPassword({ username }, updateFormType) {
  try {
    await Auth.forgotPassword(username)
    updateFormType('forgotPasswordSubmit')
  } catch (err) {
    console.log('error submitting username to reset password...', err)
  }
}

async function forgotPasswordSubmit(
    { username, confirmationCode, password }, updateFormType
  ) {
  try {
    await Auth.forgotPasswordSubmit(username, confirmationCode, password)
    updateFormType('signIn')
  } catch (err) {
    console.log('error updating password... :', err)
  }
}
```

The signUp, confirmSignUp, forgotPassword, and forgotPasswordSubmit functions will all take the same arguments, the form state object, and the updateFormType function to update the type of form that is displayed.

The signIn function is different than the other functions in that it takes in a setUser function. This setUser function will be passed into the Form component as a prop from the Profile component. This setUser function will allow us to re-render the Profile component in order to show or hide the form once the user has successfully signed in.

In Chapter 4, the *Profile.js* component used the withAuthenticator component to render the form, so we did not need to render the proper UI ourselves. Now that we are handling our own form state, we will need to decide whether to render the `Pro file` component or the `Form` component based on whether the user is authenticated.

You'll notice that in these functions we are using different methods on the `Auth` class from AWS Amplify. These methods correspond with the naming of the functions we've created so that we know exactly what each of these functions is doing.

updateForm Helper Function

Next, let's create a *helper function* for updating the form state. The initial form state variable that we created in *Form.js* looks like this:

```
const initialFormState = {
  username: '', password: '', email: '', confirmationCode: ''
}
```

This state is an object with values for each form that we will be using.

We then used this `initialFormState` variable to create the component state (as well as a function to update the component state) using the `useState` hook:

```
const [formState, updateFormState] = useState(initialFormState)
```

The problem that we have now is that `updateFormState` is expecting a new object with all of these fields in order to update the form state, but a form handler only gives us the single form event that is being typed. How can we transform this input event into a new object for the state? We'll do this by creating a helper function that we will use inside of the `Form` function.

In *Form.js*, add the following code below the `useState` hooks and inside the `Form` function:

```
function updateForm(event) {
  const newFormState = {
    ...formState, [event.target.name]: event.target.value
  }
  updateFormState(newFormState)
}
```

The `updateForm` function will create a new `state` object using the existing state as well as the new values coming in from the event and then call `updateFormState` with this new form object. We can then reuse this function across all of our components.

renderForm Function

Now that we have all of the form components created, the form state setup, and the authentication functions created, let's update the `renderForm` function to render the current form. In *Form.js*, update the `renderForm` function to use the following code:

```
function renderForm() {
  switch(formType) {
    case 'signUp':
      return (
        <SignUp
          signUp={() => signUp(formState, updateFormType)}
          updateFormState={e => updateForm(e)}
        />
      )
    case 'confirmSignUp':
      return (
        <ConfirmSignUp
          confirmSignUp={() => confirmSignUp(formState, updateFormType)}
          updateFormState={e => updateForm(e)}
        />
      )
    case 'signIn':
      return (
        <SignIn
          signIn={() => signIn(formState, props.setUser)}
          updateFormState={e => updateForm(e)}
        />
      )
    case 'forgotPassword':
      return (
        <ForgotPassword
          forgotPassword={() => forgotPassword(formState, updateFormType)}
          updateFormState={e => updateForm(e)}
        />
      )
    case 'forgotPasswordSubmit':
      return (
        <ForgotPasswordSubmit
          forgotPasswordSubmit={
            () => forgotPasswordSubmit(formState, updateFormType)}
          updateFormState={e => updateForm(e)}
        />
      )
    default:
      return null
  }
}
```

The renderForm function will check the current formType that is set in the state and render the proper form. As the formType changes, renderForm will be called and subsequently re-render the correct form based on the formType.

Form Type Toggles

The last thing we will need to do in this component is render the buttons that will allow us to manually toggle between different form states. The three main form states that we will want to toggle between are signIn, signUp, and forgotPassword.

To do this, let's update the return statement from the Form function to also return some buttons that allow the user to toggle the form type:

```
return (
  <div>
    {renderForm()}
    {
      formType === 'signUp' && (
        <p style={styles.toggleForm}>
          Already have an account? <span
            style={styles.anchor}
            onClick={() => updateFormType('signIn')}
          >Sign In</span>
        </p>
      )
    }
    {
      formType === 'signIn' && (
        <>
          <p style={styles.toggleForm}>
            Need an account? <span
              style={styles.anchor}
              onClick={() => updateFormType('signUp')}
            >Sign Up</span>
          </p>
          <p style={{ ...styles.toggleForm, ...styles.resetPassword}}>
            Forget your password? <span
              style={styles.anchor}
              onClick={() => updateFormType('forgotPassword')}
            >Reset Password</span>
          </p>
        </>
      )
    }
  </div>
)
```

The Form component will now show different buttons based on the current form type and allow the user to toggle between signing in, signing up, and resetting their password.

Updating the Profile Component

We now need to update the Profile component to use the new Form component. The main changes are that we will be rendering either the Form component or the user profile information based on whether there is a currently signed-in user.

Amplify has a local eventing system called Hub. Amplify uses Hub for different categories to communicate with one another when specific events occur, such as authentication events like a user sign-in or notification of a file download.

In this component, we will also be setting a Hub listener to listen for the signOut authentication event so that we can remove the user from the state and re-render the Profile component to show the authentication form.

Update *Profile.js* with the following code:

```
import React, { useState, useEffect } from 'react'
import { Button } from 'antd'
import { Auth, Hub } from 'aws-amplify'
import Container from './Container'
import Form from './Form'

function Profile() {
  useEffect(() => {
    checkUser()
    Hub.listen('auth', (data) => {
      const { payload } = data
      if (payload.event === 'signOut') {
        setUser(null)
      }
    })
  }, [])
  const [user, setUser] = useState(null)
  async function checkUser() {
    try {
      const data = await Auth.currentUserPoolUser()
      const userInfo = { username: data.username, ...data.attributes, }
      setUser(userInfo)
    } catch (err) { console.log('error: ', err) }
  }
  function signOut() {
    Auth.signOut()
      .catch(err => console.log('error signing out: ', err))
  }
  if (user) {
    return (
      <Container>
        <h1>Profile</h1>
        <h2>Username: {user.username}</h2>
        <h3>Email: {user.email}</h3>
        <h4>Phone: {user.phone_number}</h4>
```

```
        <Button onClick={signOut}>Sign Out</Button>
      </Container>
    );
  }
  return <Form setUser={setUser} />
}

export default Profile
```

In this component, we check to see if there is a user, and if so we return the profile information of the user. If there is no user, then we return the authentication form (Form). We pass in `setUser` as a prop to the `Form` component so that when a user signs in we can update the form state to re-render the component and show the profile information for that user.

Testing the App

To test the app, we can now run the `start` command:

```
npm start
```

Summary

Congratulations, you've built out a completely custom authentication flow!

Here are a few things to keep in mind from this chapter:

- Use the `Auth` class for handling direct API calls to the Amazon Cognito authentication service.

- As you can see, handling custom form state can become verbose. Try to understand the trade-offs between rolling your own authentication flow versus using something like the `withAuthenticator` HOC.

- Authentication is complex. By using a managed-identity service like Amazon Cognito, we've abstracted away all of the backend code and logic. The only thing we have to know or understand is how to interact with the authentication APIs and then manage the local state.

## CHAPTER 6

Serverless Functions In-Depth: Part 1

In Chapter 2, you learned how to create and interact with a serverless API using API Gateway and AWS Lambda. Here, you'll continue to learn about how to use serverless functions by creating two new types of functions. The functions in this chapter will be different in that, instead of using them as strictly a web server or an API, you'll be using them to interact with other AWS services to aid in the application-development process.

You'll be creating the following two kinds of functions in this chapter:

A function that dynamically adds a user to a group based on their email address
> In some applications, you will need to perform "coarse-grained" access control, which typically means granting certain permissions to users in a broad way based on the type of role or group they are associated with. In our example, we'll have an administrator group of users that will be identified by their email address. If a user signs up with one of these email addresses, we will place them in a group called *Admin*.

A function that automatically resizes an image after it has been uploaded to Amazon S3
> Many applications require dynamic image resizing on the server after a user has uploaded an image. This is done for many reasons, ranging from the need to make the web application more performant by compressing images to the need to dynamically create avatars or thumbnail images of a smaller size for images.

In Chapter 7, we'll continue learning about serverless functions by creating an ecommerce application that interacts with a database and allows the user to create, read, update, and delete items from a database by invoking the function via an API call.

Event Sources and Data Structure

In Chapter 2, we briefly talked about event sources for serverless functions as part of an event-based architecture. The only event source we have implemented up until this point has been from API Gateway: an HTTP request that triggered the function, and fetched data from an API and returned it in the response. In this chapter, we'll be working with two other event types and sources, one from Amazon S3 and one from Amazon Cognito.

To understand the events coming into Lambda from the event sources, it's important to underscore the following point: the shape of the event data will differ between different event types. For instance, the HTTP event data structure coming from API Gateway will be different than the Amazon S3 event data structure, and the Amazon S3 event data structure will differ from the Amazon Cognito data structure.

Understanding the shape of the event data, as well as knowing the data available to you in the event, will help you understand the capabilities of what you can do in the Lambda function. To understand this better, let's take a look at the shape of various data structures from different events. For now, you do not need to understand every field and value in these data structures. I will outline the values that will be important for us in the following examples.

API Gateway Event

The API gateway event data is the data structure that will be passed into the Lambda function when invoking it from an API Gateway HTTP event, like GET, PUT, POST, or DELETE. This data structure holds information like the HTTP method that invoked the function, the path that was invoked, the body if one was passed in, and the identity of the user calling the API (inside the `requestContext.identity` field) if the user was authenticated:

```
{
    "resource": "/items",
    "path": "/items",
    "httpMethod": "GET",
    "headers": { /* header info */ },
    "multiValueHeaders": { /* multi value header info */ },
    "queryStringParameters": null,
    "multiValueQueryStringParameters": null,
    "pathParameters": null,
    "stageVariables": null,
    "requestContext": {
        "resourceId": "b16tgj",
        "resourcePath": "/items",
        "httpMethod": "GET",
        "extendedRequestId": "CzuJMEDMoAMF_MQ=",
        "requestTime": "07/Nov/2019:21:46:09 +0000",
```

```
        "path": "/dev/items",
        "accountId": "557458351015",
        "protocol": "HTTP/1.1",
        "stage": "dev",
        "domainPrefix": "eq4ttnl94k",
        "requestTimeEpoch": 1573163169162,
        "requestId": "1ac70afe-d366-4a52-9329-5fcbcc3809d8",
        "identity": {
          "cognitoIdentityPoolId": "",
          "accountId": "",
          "cognitoIdentityId": "",
          "caller": "",
          "apiKey": "",
          "sourceIp": "192.168.100.1",
          "cognitoAuthenticationType": "",
          "cognitoAuthenticationProvider": "",
          "userArn": "",
          "userAgent": "Mozilla/5.0 (Macintosh; Intel Mac OS X 10_11_6)
          AppleWebKit/537.36 (KHTML, like Gecko) Chrome/52.0.2743.82
          Safari/537.36 OPR/39.0.2256.48",
          "user": ""
        },
        "domainName": "eq4ttnl94k.execute-api.us-east-1.amazonaws.com",
        "apiId": "eq4ttnl94k"
    },
    "body": null,
    "isBase64Encoded": false
}
```

Amazon S3 Event

The Amazon S3 event is the data structure that will be received when invoking a
Lambda function from a file upload or update to Amazon S3. This data structure
holds an array of records from S3. The main information you'll typically be working
with in this event data is the s3 field. This property holds information like the bucket
name, the key, and the size of the item being stored:

```
{
  "Records": [
    {
      "eventVersion": "2.1",
      "eventSource": "aws:s3",
      "awsRegion": "us-east-2",
      "eventTime": "2019-09-03T19:37:27.192Z",
      "eventName": "ObjectCreated:Put",
      "userIdentity": {
        "principalId": "AWS:AIDAINPONIXQXHT3IKHL2"
      },
      "requestParameters": {
        "sourceIPAddress": "205.255.255.255"
      },
```

```
    "responseElements": {
      "x-amz-request-id": "D82B88E5F771F645",
      "x-amz-id-2": "vlR7PnpV2Ce81l0PRw6jlUpck7Jo5ZsQjryTjKlc5aLWGVHPZLj
                     5NeC6qMa0emYBDXOo6QBU0Wo="
    },
    "s3": {
      "s3SchemaVersion": "1.0",
      "configurationId": "828aa6fc-f7b5-4305-8584-487c791949c1",
      "bucket": {
        "name": "lambda-artifacts-deafc19498e3f2df",
        "ownerIdentity": {
          "principalId": "A3I5XTEXAMAI3E"
        },
        "arn": "arn:aws:s3:::lambda-artifacts-deafc19498e3f2df"
      },
      "object": {
        "key": "b21b84d653bb07b05b1e6b33684dc11b",
        "size": 1305107,
        "eTag": "b21b84d653bb07b05b1e6b33684dc11b",
        "sequencer": "0C0F6F405D6ED209E1"
      }
    }
  }
 ]
}
```

Amazon Cognito Event

The Amazon Cognito event data is the data structure that will be passed into the
function when being invoked from an Amazon Cognito action. These actions could
be anything from a user signing up, a user confirming their account, or a user signing
in, among other available events:

```
{
    "version": "1",
    "region": "us-east-1",
    "userPoolId": "us-east-1_uVWAMpQuY",
    "userName": "dabit3",
    "callerContext": {
        "awsSdkVersion": "aws-sdk-unknown-unknown",
        "clientId": "2ects9inqraapp43ejve80pv12"
    },
    "triggerSource": "PostConfirmation_ConfirmSignUp",
    "request": {
        "userAttributes": {
            "sub": "164961f8-13f7-40ed-a8ca-d441d8ec4724",
            "cognito:user_status": "CONFIRMED",
            "email_verified": "true",
            "phone_number_verified": "false",
            "phone_number": "+16018127241",
            "email": "dabit3@gmail.com"
        }
```

```
    },
    "response": {}
}
```

You'll be using these events and the information contained within them to perform different types of actions from within the functions.

IAM Permissions and Trigger Configuration

When setting up these triggers using the CLI, a couple of things are happening under the hood:

- The CLI is enabling the trigger itself in the Lambda configuration. When a trigger is enabled, the event will be sent to the function every time that interaction happens (API event, S3 upload, etc.).
- The CLI is giving additional permissions to the function itself to interact with other services. For instance, when we enable the S3 trigger in this chapter, we are wanting the Lambda function to be able to read and store images in that bucket.

  To enable this, the CLI will add additional Identity and Access Management (IAM) policies under the hood to the function, giving it permissions like read and write access to work with S3, or permissions to interact with the Cognito user pool in our other example.

Creating the Base Project

The first thing we'll do is create a new React application and install the dependencies we'll need for this chapter:

```
~ npx create-react-app lambda-trigger-example
~ cd lambda-trigger-example
~ npm install aws-amplify @aws-amplify/ui-react uuid
```

Next, we'll create a new Amplify project:

```
~ amplify init
# walk through the steps like we've done in the previous projects
```

Now that the project has been initialized, we can begin adding the services. The services we'll need for this chapter will be Amazon Cognito, Amazon S3, and AWS Lambda. We'll start by adding Amazon Cognito and testing out a post-confirmation Lambda trigger.

Adding a Post-Confirmation Lambda Trigger

The next thing we want to do is create an authentication service. We will then create and configure a post-confirmation Lambda trigger. This means we want a Lambda function to be invoked every time someone successfully signs up and confirms their account using our authentication service. This post-confirmation trigger only fires once per confirmed user:

```
~ amplify add auth

? Do you want to use the default authentication and security configuration?
  Default configuration
? How do you want users to be able to sign in? Username
? Do you want to configure advanced settings? Yes
? What attributes are required for signing up? Email
? Do you want to enable any of the following capabilities? Add User to Group
? Enter the name of the group to which users will be added. Admin
? Do you want to edit your add-to-group function now? Y
```

Now, update the function with the following code:

```
// amplify/backend/function/<function_name>/src/add-to-group.js

const aws = require('aws-sdk');

exports.handler = async (event, context, callback) => {
  const cognitoProvider = new
  aws.CognitoIdentityServiceProvider({
    apiVersion: '2016-04-18'
  });

  let isAdmin = false
  const adminEmails = ['dabit3@gmail.com']

  // If the user is one of the admins, set the isAdmin variable to true
  if (adminEmails.indexOf(event.request.userAttributes.email) !== -1) {
    isAdmin = true
  }

  const groupParams = {
    UserPoolId: event.userPoolId,
  }

  const userParams = {
    UserPoolId: event.userPoolId,
    Username: event.userName,
  }

  if (isAdmin) {
    groupParams.GroupName = 'Admin',
    userParams.GroupName = 'Admin'
```

```
    // First check to see if the group exists, and if not create the group
    try {
      await cognitoProvider.getGroup(groupParams).promise();
    } catch (e) {
      await cognitoProvider.createGroup(groupParams).promise();
    }

    // If the user is an administrator, place them in the Admin group
    try {
      await cognitoProvider.adminAddUserToGroup(userParams).promise();
      callback(null, event);
    } catch (e) {
      callback(e);
    }
  } else {
    // If the user is in neither group, proceed with no action
    callback(null, event)
  }
}
```

In this function, there is one main piece of functionality. If the user is one of the admins specified in the `admins` email array, we automatically place them in the group called `Admins`. Change the values in the `adminEmails` array to include your email address.

To deploy the service, run the push command:

```
~ amplify push
```

Now that the backend is set up, we can test it out. To do so, we first need to configure the React project to recognize the Amplify dependencies. Open *src/index.js* and add the following below the last import:

```
import Amplify from 'aws-amplify'
import config from './aws-exports'
Amplify.configure(config)
```

Next, we'll sign up a new user and display a greeting if they are an admin. To do so, open *src/App.js* and add the following:

```
import React, { useEffect, useState } from 'react'
import { Auth } from 'aws-amplify'
import { withAuthenticator, AmplifySignOut } from '@aws-amplify/ui-react'
import './App.css'

function App() {
  const [user, updateUser] = useState(null)
  useEffect(() => {
    Auth.currentAuthenticatedUser()
      .then(user => updateUser(user))
      .catch(err => console.log(err));
  }, [])
  let isAdmin = false
```

```
    if (user) {
      const { signInUserSession: { idToken: { payload }} }  = user
      console.log('payload: ', payload)
      if (
        payload['cognito:groups'] &&
      payload['cognito:groups'].includes('Admin')
      ) {
        isAdmin = true
      }
    }
    return (
      <div className="App">
        <header>
        <h1>Hello World</h1>
        { isAdmin && <p>Welcome, Admin</p> }
        </header>
        <AmplifySignOut />
      </div>
    );
  }

  export default withAuthenticator(App)
```

Run the app:

```
~ npm start
```

Now, sign up with an admin user. If the user is indeed one of the admins, you should see the Welcome, Admin greeting.

You can also view the Amazon Cognito authentication service and all of the users and groups by running the following command:

```
~ amplify console auth

? Which console: User Pool

> In the left hand menu, click on "Users and Groups"
```

Dynamic Image Resizing with AWS Lambda and Amazon S3

In the next example, we will add functionality that allows users to upload images to Amazon S3. We'll also configure an S3 trigger to call a Lambda function every time a file is uploaded to the bucket. In this function, we'll check the size of the image, and if it is above a certain width, we will resize it to be below the width threshold.

For this to work, we need to enable S3 to trigger the Lambda function in our project when a file is uploaded. We can do this using the Amplify CLI by just creating the S3 bucket and choosing the correct configuration. From the CLI, run the following commands:

```
~ amplify add storage

? Please select from one of the below mentioned services: Content
? Please provide a friendly name for your resource that will be used to label
  this category in the project: <your_resource_name>
? Please provide bucket name: <your_globally_unique_bucket_name>
? Who should have access: Auth and Guest users
? What kind of access do you want for Authenticated users? Choose all
  (create / update, read, & delete)
? What kind of access do you want for Guest users? Choose all
  (create / update, read, & delete)
? Do you want to add a Lambda Trigger for your S3 Bucket? Y
? Select from the following options: Create a new function
? Do you want to edit the local S3Trigger18399e19 lambda function now? Y
```

This will open the function into your text editor.

Adding the Custom Logic for Resizing the Image

Now, we can update the function to implement the image resizing.

In this function, we will fetch the image from S3 when the event comes through, and check to see if it is greater than 1,000 pixels wide. If that's the case, then we'll resize it to 1,000 pixels wide and save it back to the S3 bucket. If the image is not larger than 1,000 pixels wide, we exit from the function without taking any action:

```
// amplify/backend/function/<functionname>/src/index.js

// Import the sharp library
const sharp = require('sharp')
const aws = require('aws-sdk')
const s3 = new aws.S3()

exports.handler = async function (event, context) { //eslint-disable-line
  // If the event type is delete, return from the function
  if (event.Records[0].eventName === 'ObjectRemoved:Delete') return

  // Next, we get the bucket name and the key from the event.
  const BUCKET = event.Records[0].s3.bucket.name
  const KEY = event.Records[0].s3.object.key
  try {
    // Fetch the image data from S3
    let image = await s3.getObject({ Bucket: BUCKET, Key: KEY }).promise()
    image = await sharp(image.Body)

    // Get the metadata from the image, including the width and the height
    const metadata = await image.metadata()
    if (metadata.width > 1000) {
      // If the width is greater than 1000, the image is resized
```

```
        const resizedImage = await image.resize({ width: 1000 }).toBuffer()
        await s3.putObject({
          Bucket: BUCKET,
          Body: resizedImage,
          Key: KEY
        }).promise()
        return
      } else {
        return
      }
    }
    catch(err) {
      context.fail(`Error getting files: ${err}`);
    }
  };
```

For our function to work, we need to do one more thing. We are requiring the Sharp library in our Lambda function, but so far we have not installed this dependency. To make sure this module is installed, update the *package.json* file for the function to add both the dependency for the package as well as an install script that we will need in order for Sharp to run correctly in the Lambda environment. The two fields we will be adding are scripts and dependencies:

```
// amplify/backend/function/<functionname>/src/package.json
{
  "name": "your-function-name",
  "version": "2.0.0",
  "description": "Lambda function generated by Amplify",
  "main": "index.js",
  "license": "Apache-2.0",
  "scripts": {
    "install": "npm install --arch=x64 --platform=linux sharp"
  },
  "dependencies": {
    "sharp": "^0.23.2"
  }
}
```

Now, the service is ready to be deployed:

```
~ amplify push
```

Uploading Images from the React Application

Next, open *src/App.js* and add the following code to render an image picker and photo list:

```
import React, { useState, useEffect} from 'react'
import { Storage } from 'aws-amplify'
import { v4 as uuid } from 'uuid'
import './App.css'
```

```
function App() {
  const [images, setImages] = useState([])
  useEffect(() => {
    fetchImages()
  }, [])
  async function onChange(e) {
    /* When a file is uploaded, create a unique name and save it using
       the Storage API */
    const file = e.target.files[0];
    const filetype = file.name.split('.')[file.name.split.length - 1]
    await Storage.put(`${uuid()}.${filetype}`, file)
    /* Once the file is uploaded, fetch the list of images */
    fetchImages()
  }
  async function fetchImages() {
    /* This function fetches the list of image keys from your S3 bucket */
    const files = await Storage.list('')
    /* Once we have the image keys, the images must be signed in order
       for them to be displayed */
    const signedFiles = await Promise.all(files.map(async file => {
      /* To sign the images, we map over the image key array and get a
         signed url for each image */
      const signedFile = await Storage.get(file.key)
      return signedFile
    }))
    setImages(signedFiles)
  }

  return (
    <div className="App">
      <header className="App-header">
        <input
          type="file"
          onChange={onChange}
        />
        {
          images.map(image => (
            <img
              src={image}
              key={image}
              style={{ width: 500 }}
            />
          ))
        }
      </header>
    </div>
  );
}

export default App
```

Next, run the app:

```
~ npm start
```

When you upload an image that is wider than 1,000 pixels, you'll notice that it will initially load as the original size, but if you reload the app, you will see that the image has been resized to the correct 1,000-pixel width.

Summary

Congratulations, you've now successfully implemented two types of Lambda triggers!

Here are a few things to keep in mind from this chapter:

- Lambda functions can be invoked from many different event types, including API calls, image uploads, database operations, and authentication events.
- The event data structure differs based on the type of event invoking the Lambda function.
- Understanding the data available in the event variable enables you to better evaluate the things that can be accomplished within the function.
- When a Lambda trigger is enabled by the Amplify CLI, additional IAM permissions are given to the function, allowing it to directly interact with other services.

## CHAPTER 7

Serverless Functions In-Depth: Part 2

So far, we have covered quite a bit of functionality that can be achieved using a Lambda function. In this chapter, we'll continue learning how to use Lambda functions in different ways to implement common functionality you'll find useful when building applications. We'll get into how to create and integrate into our app a fully functional backend complete with an API, authentication, a database, and authorization rules.

With Amplify, there are two main ways to create APIs: GraphQL and REST. We'll continue to cover GraphQL in Chapter 8, but here, we'll learn how to do this with a REST API running in a Lambda function.

The database we will use is Amazon DynamoDB, a NoSQL database. We will be invoking the Lambda function from an HTTP request routed through an API gateway endpoint. The Lambda function will take the HTTP request and then route it to different paths as the function will be running an Express web server.

This will allow us to have different routes available within a single function. We will then map different HTTP methods, like `post` and `delete`, to the routes to perform different actions on the database.

What We'll Build

We'll be building a basic ecommerce app that allows users to view products, and administrators to create and delete products. The building blocks of this app will lay the groundwork for building almost any type of CRUD+L (create, read, update, delete, and list) application, which is the backbone of many real-world projects.

We will be using what we learned in Chapters 2 and 6 and building upon those ideas in this chapter.

The services and features we'll be needing are the following:

Lambda function
> The main application logic will reside in a Lambda function that will be running an Express server. The server will have routes for the different HTTP methods we will need to work with: `get`, `post`, and `delete`.

API
> In order to interact with the main Lambda function, we will need to be able to invoke it using HTTP requests, sending `get`, `post`, and `delete` requests to interact with the API and the database.

DynamoDB NoSQL Database
> This is the database that will hold all of the data for the application.

Authentication
> We will need a way to authenticate users in order to configure and enable administrator access.

Another Lambda function
> We will need a Lambda trigger to place administrators into an Admin group, so there will be another Lambda function (post-confirmation trigger) associated with the authentication flow.

Like in previous chapters, we will need to integrate navigation into the client application for linking between routes. When a user is signed in, we will access the user's groups to determine the state of the app based on the user's permissions. These permissions might include determining whether or not to show the Admin navigation link or to allow users to view the buttons to delete items based on whether they are an administrator or not.

We will also have some authorization guards on the server to make sure that if a user performs an action, that they are indeed authorized to perform that action.

Getting Started

The first thing we will need to do to get started is to create a new React application and install the necessary dependencies:

```
~ npx create-react-app ecommerceapp

~ cd ecommerceapp

~ npm install aws-amplify @aws-amplify/ui-react react-router-dom antd
```

Next, we will initialize a new Amplify project and begin adding the services we'll need for this application:

```
~ amplify init

# Follow the steps to give the project a name, environment name, and
  set the default text editor.
# Accept defaults for everything else and choose your AWS Profile.
```

Adding Authentication and Group Privileges

The first service we'll create is the authentication service. We need to be sure to also create the Lambda trigger in order to add users to the Admin group that we will be creating:

```
~ amplify add auth

? Do you want to use the default authentication and security configuration?
  Default configuration
? How do you want users to be able to sign in? Username
? Do you want to configure advanced settings? Yes
? What attributes are required for signing up? Email
? Do you want to enable any of the following capabilities? Add User to Group
? Enter the name of the group to which users will be added. Admin
? Do you want to edit your add-to-group function now? Y
```

Update the function with the following code and configure the adminEmails array:

```
// amplify/backend/function/<function_name>/src/add-to-group.js
const aws = require('aws-sdk');

exports.handler = async (event, context, callback) => {
  const cognitoProvider = new
  aws.CognitoIdentityServiceProvider({
    apiVersion: '2016-04-18'
  });

  let isAdmin = false
  // Update this array to include any admin emails you would like to enable
  const adminEmails = ['dabit3@gmail.com']

  // If the user is one of the admins, set the isAdmin variable to true
  if (adminEmails.indexOf(event.request.userAttributes.email) !== -1) {
    isAdmin = true
  }

  if (isAdmin) {
    const groupParams = {
      UserPoolId: event.userPoolId,
      GroupName: 'Admin'
    }
    const userParams = {
      UserPoolId: event.userPoolId,
      Username: event.userName,
      GroupName: 'Admin'
```

```
    }
    // First check to see if the group exists, and if not create the group
    try {
      await cognitoProvider.getGroup(groupParams).promise();
    } catch (e) {
      await cognitoProvider.createGroup(groupParams).promise();
    }
    // The user is an administrator, place them in the Admin group
    try {
      await cognitoProvider.adminAddUserToGroup(userParams).promise();
      callback(null, event);
    } catch (e) { callback(e); }
  } else {
    // If the user is in neither group, proceed with no action
    callback(null, event)
  }
}
```

In this function, we set an array of admin emails and an `isAdmin` variable. If the confirmed user is an admin, we first check to see if the Admin group has already created in the service. If it has not yet been created, we create it.

We then add the user to the group by calling `cognitoProvider.adminAddUser ToGroup`, passing in the parameters.

Adding the Database

Next, we will create the DynamoDB NoSQL database for the project. To add the database, we can use the `Storage` category:

```
~ amplify add storage

? Please select from one of the below mentioned services: NoSQL Database
? Please provide a friendly name for your resource that will be used to label
  this category in the project: producttable
? Please provide table name: producttable
? What would you like to name this column: id
? Please choose the data type: string
? Would you like to add another column? N
? Please choose partition key for the table: id
? Do you want to add a sort key to your table? N
? Do you want to add global secondary indexes to your table? N
? Do you want to add a Lambda Trigger for your Table? N
```

When working with DynamoDB, you have to have either a unique *primary key* or a unique combination of primary and *sort key* to uniquely identify individual items in the database. In our database, we have a primary key of `id` that will be the unique identifier for the items in the database.

There is also an option on the table to create *global secondary indexes* (GSIs). These allow us to add additional indexes that can be used to query our table and enable additional data access patterns. One of the most powerful features of DynamoDB and NoSQL databases in general is the idea of having other indexes (up to 20 GSIs for DynamoDB) that enable a multitude of access patterns. We will not be utilizing any secondary indexes hre, but I encourage you to look into how this works to further your knowledge of how to maximize the power and flexibility of DynamoDB.

Adding the API

Now that the database has been created, we'll now create an API and another Lambda function that will interact with the database:

```
~ amplify add api

? Please select from one of the below mentioned services: REST
? Provide a friendly name for your resource to be used as a label for this
  category in the project: ecommerceapi
? Provide a path: /products
? Choose a Lambda source: Create a new Lambda function
? Provide a friendly name for your resource to be used as a label for this
  category in the project: ecommercefunction
? Provide the AWS Lambda function name: ecommercefunction
? Choose the function runtime that you want to use: NodeJS
? Choose the function template that you want to use: Serverless express
  function (Integration with Amazon API Gateway)
? Do you want to access other resources created in this project from your
  Lambda function? Y
? Select the category: storage, auth
? Select the operations you want to permit for <app_name>: create, read, update,
  delete
? Select the operations you want to permit for producttable: create, read,
  update, delete
? Do you want to invoke this function on a recurring schedule? N
? Do you want to configure Lambda layers for this function? N
? Do you want to edit the local Lambda function now? N
? Restrict API access: Y
? Who should have access? Authenticated and Guest users
? What kind of access do you want for Authenticated users? create, read,
  update, delete
? What kind of access do you want for Guest users? read
? Do you want to add another path? N
```

Now we've created an API Gateway endpoint as well as a new Lambda function and integrated the function to be triggered from the API Gateway event. The CLI walks us through the setup, and allows us to set some base authorization rules around the API by restricting API access based on whether the user is authenticated or not. We've also set up a path that we will now be able to work with: /products.

The Lambda function includes an Express server as part of the boilerplate the CLI created for us. If you haven't used Express before, it is a minimal Node.js web framework that provides a nice set of built-in features to develop web and mobile applications. For our purposes, we will be using it to more easily provide routing that will map to the endpoint(s) that we create in API Gateway. We'll now be able to have get, put, post, and delete methods that we can call on the /products endpoint that will be handled by the Express framework.

If we wanted to add additional endpoints, we could update the api category by running amplify update api and then adding whatever new endpoints we'd created directly into the Express server code.

Next, we will go ahead and update the code in the Lambda function that is running the Express server to handle the interactions with the database that we'd like to enable.

The first thing we need to do is update the imports for the function:

```
/* amplify/backend/function/ecommercefunction/src/app.js */

/* Below the last existing `require` import, add the following
    imports variables */
const AWS = require('aws-sdk')
const { v4: uuid } = require('uuid')

/* Cognito SDK */
const cognito = new
AWS.CognitoIdentityServiceProvider({
  apiVersion: '2016-04-18'
})

/* Cognito User Pool ID
* This User Pool ID variable will be given to you by the CLI output after
    adding the category
* This will also be available in the file itself, commented out at the top
*/
var userpoolId = process.env.<your_app_id>

// DynamoDB configuration
const region = process.env.REGION
const ddb_table_name = process.env.STORAGE_PRODUCTTABLE_NAME
const docClient = new AWS.DynamoDB.DocumentClient({region})
```

Next, we'll create a couple of functions that will allow us to perform authorization checks on the API call. We want only users in the Admin group to be able to perform certain actions (while leaving open the potential to allow other groups in future).

To do this, we will create two functions: getGroupsForUser and canPerformAction:

getGroupsForUser

This will allow us to pass in the event coming in from the API call to determine what groups the user making the call is currently associated with.

canPerformAction

This first checks to see if the user is authenticated at all, and if not, will reject the request. It will then check to see if the user is part of the group passed in as the second argument, and if so, will allow the action to happen. If not, it will reject the action.

Create the functions with the following code:

```
// amplify/backend/function/ecommercefunction/src/app.js
async function getGroupsForUser(event) {
  let userSub =
    event
      .requestContext
      .identity
      .cognitoAuthenticationProvider
      .split(':CognitoSignIn:')[1]
  let userParams = {
    UserPoolId: userpoolId,
    Filter: `sub = "${userSub}"`,
  }
  let userData = await cognito.listUsers(userParams).promise()
  const user = userData.Users[0]
  var groupParams = {
    UserPoolId: userpoolId,
    Username: user.Username
  }
  const groupData = await cognito.adminListGroupsForUser(groupParams).promise()
  return groupData
}

async function canPerformAction(event, group) {
  return new Promise(async (resolve, reject) => {
    if (!event.requestContext.identity.cognitoAuthenticationProvider) {
      return reject()
    }
    const groupData = await getGroupsForUser(event)
    const groupsForUser = groupData.Groups.map(group => group.GroupName)
    if (groupsForUser.includes(group)) {
      resolve()
    } else {
      reject('user not in group, cannot perform action..')
    }
  })
}
```

Next, we will update the HTTP methods of `get`, `post`, and `delete` to interact with the database.

Let's first update `app.get` for `/products`:

```
// amplify/backend/function/ecommercefunction/src/app.js
app.get('/products', async function(req, res) {
  try {
    const data = await getItems()
    res.json({ data: data })
  } catch (err) {
    res.json({ error: err })
  }
})

async function getItems(){
  var params = { TableName: ddb_table_name }
  try {
    const data = await docClient.scan(params).promise()
    return data
  } catch (err) {
    return err
  }
}
```

This method calls a new function that we create named `getItems` that fetches the items from the DynamoDB table using a scan operation (`docClient.scan`). If the scan operation succeeds, we return the items in the response. If the operation fails, we return the error message.

Next, let's update `app.post` for `/products` to see how to create a new item in DynamoDB:

```
// amplify/backend/function/ecommercefunction/src/app.js
app.post('/products', async function(req, res) {
  const { body } = req
  const { event } = req.apiGateway
  try {
    await canPerformAction(event, 'Admin')
    const input = { ...body, id: uuid() }
    var params = {
      TableName: ddb_table_name,
      Item: input
    }
    await docClient.put(params).promise()
    res.json({ success: 'item saved to database..' })
  } catch (err) {
    res.json({ error: err })
  }
});
```

This call is a little different than the get call. You can see that we retrieve the body from the event using the req object and then get event data from the req.apiGateway object.

We first call canPerformAction to see if the caller is an admin. If this succeeds, we continue on to create an input object using the body argument and appending a unique ID onto the object.

We then create a new params variable that contains the input along with the table name. Finally, we call the put method using the DynamoDB Document Client to create a new item.

Next, let's look at how to delete an item by updating the app.delete method for /products:

```
// amplify/backend/function/ecommercefunction/src/app.js
app.delete('/products', async function(req, res) {
  const { event } = req.apiGateway
  try {
    await canPerformAction(event, 'Admin')
    var params = {
      TableName : ddb_table_name,
      Key: { id: req.body.id }
    }
    await docClient.delete(params).promise()
    res.json({ success: 'successfully deleted item' })
  } catch (err) {
    res.json({ error: err })
  }
});
```

The delete method, like the post method, requires an admin to perform the action. To implement this, we first check if they are an admin by calling canPerformAction. We then call the delete method using the DynamoDB Document Client to delete an item by passing in the primary key of id.

Finally, because we used the uuid library in our function, we will need to add it as a dependency to the function's *package.json* file. In *amplify/backend/function/ecommercefunction/src/package.json*, add uuid as a dependency:

```
{
  ...
  "dependencies": {
    "aws-serverless-express": "^3.3.5",
    "body-parser": "^1.17.1",
    "express": "^4.15.2",
    "uuid": "^8.0.0" <- New dependency
  },
  ...
}
```

Now, the backend has been set up and we can deploy it to AWS:

```
~ amplify push
```

Creating the Frontend

The first thing we'll do on the frontend is create the files we'll need to work with:

Admin.js
> This component will hold the Admin dashboard to create new items.

Container.js
> This will be a reusable layout component.

Main.js
> This holds the main view of the app that will list the items that are for sale being pulled from the API and database.

Nav.js
> This will hold the navigation component.

Profile.js
> This will be a basic profile component that will allow users to sign out.

Router.js
> This component will hold the router.

checkUser.js
> This will hold a function that will retrieve the user's profile and determine whether the user is an admin.

Let's next go ahead and change into the *src* directory and create these components:

```
~ cd src
~ touch Admin.js Container.js Main.js Nav.js Profile.js Router.js checkUser.js
~ cd ..
```

Next, open *src/index.js* and update it with the following code to import the Router, the Amplify library, and the CSS from Ant Design:

```
import React from 'react'
import ReactDOM from 'react-dom'
import Router from './Router'

import 'antd/dist/antd.css'
import Amplify from 'aws-amplify'
import config from './aws-exports'
Amplify.configure(config)

ReactDOM.render(<Router />, document.getElementById('root'))
```

Container Component

The `Container` component will provide a basic layout with a fixed width and center the components in a consistent way:

```
import React from 'react'

export default function Container({ children }) {
  return (
    <div style={containerStyle}>
      {children}
    </div>
  )
}

const containerStyle = {
  width: 900,
  margin: '0 auto',
  padding: '20px 0px'
}
```

checkUser Function

This function will check the current user's information and then call the `updateUser` callback function to update the user. If there is no user, it returns with an empty object.

If there is a user, it will check to see if there are any Cognito groups associated with the user, and if so, check if the user is in the `Admin` group. If the user is in the `Admin` group, then the `isAuthorized` Boolean will be set to `true`; if not, the Boolean will be set to `false`:

```
/* src/checkUser.js */
import { Auth } from 'aws-amplify'

async function checkUser(updateUser) {
  const userData = await Auth
    .currentSession()
    .catch(err => console.log('error: ', err)
  )
  if (!userData) {
    console.log('userData: ', userData)
    updateUser({})
    return
  }
  const { idToken: { payload }} = userData
  const isAuthorized =
    payload['cognito:groups'] &&
  payload['cognito:groups'].includes('Admin')
  updateUser({
    username: payload['cognito:username'],
```

```
    isAuthorized
  })
}

export default checkUser
```

Nav Component

The Nav component will hold to main links (Home and Profile), and another admin
link that will only be visible if you are signed in as an admin user:

```
/* src/Nav.js */
import React, { useState, useEffect } from 'react'
import { Link } from 'react-router-dom'
import { Menu } from 'antd'
import { HomeOutlined, UserOutlined, ProfileOutlined } from '@ant-design/icons'
import { Hub } from 'aws-amplify'
import checkUser from './checkUser'

const Nav = (props) => {
  const { current } = props
  const [user, updateUser] = useState({})
  useEffect(() => {
    checkUser(updateUser)
    Hub.listen('auth', (data) => {
      const { payload: { event } } = data;
      console.log('event: ', event)
      if (event === 'signIn' || event === 'signOut') checkUser(updateUser)
    })
  }, [])

  return (
    <div>
      <Menu selectedKeys={[current]} mode="horizontal">
        <Menu.Item key='home'>
          <Link to={`/`}>
            <HomeOutlined />Home
          </Link>
        </Menu.Item>
        <Menu.Item key='profile'>
          <Link to='/profile'>
            <UserOutlined />Profile
          </Link>
        </Menu.Item>
        {
          user.isAuthorized && (
            <Menu.Item key='admin'>
              <Link to='/admin'>
                <ProfileOutlined />Admin
              </Link>
            </Menu.Item>
          )
```

```
        }
      </Menu>
    </div>
  )
}
```

```
export default Nav
```

In this component, we use the `useEffect` hook to call the `checkUser` function when the component loads. This will set the component state with the user information if there is a signed-in user.

We also set up a listener, using the `Hub` component, to listen to `auth` events (like signing up, signing in, and signing out). When a user signs in or signs out, we again will invoke the `checkUser` function to keep the navigation state up to date.

In the user interface, we then decide to only show the `Admin` link if the user is an authorized admin user.

Profile Component

This component is pretty basic. If a user is signed in, we will render the component and a sign-out button. If they are not signed in, the `withAuthenticator` component will render sign-up and sign-in flows for a user:

```
/* src/Profile.js */
import React from 'react'
import './App.css'

import { withAuthenticator, AmplifySignOut } from '@aws-amplify/ui-react'

function Profile() {
  return (
    <div style={{containerStyle}}>
      <AmplifySignOut />
    </div>
  );
}

const containerStyle = {
  width: 400,
  margin: '20px auto'
}

export default withAuthenticator(Profile)
```

Router Component

This component configures three main components and routes: `Main` (`/`), `Admin` (`/admin`), and `Profile` (`/profile`).

In the `useEffect` hook, we first call the `setRoute` function. This function will get the current window location and set the current route information to be passed down to the `Nav` component:

```
/* src/Router.js */
import React, {useState, useEffect} from 'react'
import { HashRouter, Route, Switch } from 'react-router-dom'

import Nav from './Nav'
import Admin from './Admin'
import Main from './Main'
import Profile from './Profile'

export default function Router() {
  const [current, setCurrent] = useState('home')
  useEffect(() => {
    setRoute()
    window.addEventListener('hashchange', setRoute)
    return () => window.removeEventListener('hashchange', setRoute)
  }, [])
  function setRoute() {
    const location = window.location.href.split('/')
    const pathname = location[location.length-1]
    console.log('pathname: ', pathname)
    setCurrent(pathname ? pathname : 'home')
  }
  return (
    <HashRouter>
      <Nav current={current} />
      <Switch>
        <Route exact path='/' component={Main} />
        <Route path='/admin' component={Admin} />
        <Route path='/profile' component={Profile} />
        <Route component={Main} />
      </Switch>
    </HashRouter>
  )
}
```

We also set up a listener to listen when the route changes (`hashchange`), and when it does, we will call `setRoute` to set the current route information to be passed down to the `Nav` component.

Admin Component

The `Admin` component contains a form that will allow us to create new items in the inventory:

```
/* src/Admin.js */
import React, { useState } from 'react'
import './App.css'
import { Input, Button } from 'antd'

import { API } from 'aws-amplify'
import { withAuthenticator } from '@aws-amplify/ui-react'

const initialState = {
  name: '', price: ''
}

function Admin() {
  const [itemInfo, updateItemInfo] = useState(initialState)
  function updateForm(e) {
    const formData = {
      ...itemInfo, [e.target.name]: e.target.value
    }
    updateItemInfo(formData)
  }
  async function addItem() {
    try {
      const data = {
        body: { ...itemInfo, price: parseInt(itemInfo.price) }
      }
      updateItemInfo(initialState)
      await API.post('ecommerceapi', '/products', data)
    } catch (err) {
      console.log('error adding item...')
    }
  }
  return (
    <div style={containerStyle}>
      <Input
        name='name'
        onChange={updateForm}
        value={itemInfo.name}
        placeholder='Item name'
        style={inputStyle}
      />
      <Input
        name='price'
        onChange={updateForm}
        value={itemInfo.price}
        style={inputStyle}
        placeholder='item price'
      />
```

```
      <Button
        style={buttonStyle}
        onClick={addItem}
      >Add Product</Button>
    </div>
  )
}

const containerStyle = { width: 400, margin: '20px auto' }
const inputStyle = { marginTop: 10 }
const buttonStyle = { marginTop: 10 }

export default withAuthenticator(Admin)
```

The main thing happening in this component is the `addItem` function.

This function uses the `API` category to interact with the REST API we created. When we set up this API, we named it `ecommerceapi`. Using the API name, as well as the path (`/products`), we can make requests against it, like `get`, `put`, `post`, and `delete`.

In our component, we called `API.post`, passing in an object containing the data we wanted to send in the body:

```
/* Create the object to send with the request */
const data = {
  body: { ...itemInfo, price: parseInt(itemInfo.price) }
}
/* Update the local state with the initial state to clear the form */
updateItemInfo(initialState)
/* Post to the API */
await API.post('ecommerceapi', '/products', data)
```

Main Component

The last component is the `Main` component, which is the main view that renders the list of inventory items.

There are two main functions in this component, `getProducts` and `deleteItem`:

getProducts
: Calls the `get` method on the API. When the data is returned, the state is updated, setting the products array to the data returned from the API.

deleteItem
1. The `id` of the item to be deleted is used create a filtered list of the products array by removing the item to be deleted.

2. The filtered products array is used to update the local state, creating an optimistic response in the UI by deleting the item in the view and showing the new list of products immediately.

3. We use the API category to make a delete request, passing in the id of the product:

```
/* src/Main.js */
import React, { useState, useEffect } from 'react'
import Container from './Container'
import { API } from 'aws-amplify'
import { List } from 'antd'
import checkUser from './checkUser'

function Main() {
  const [state, setState] = useState({products: [], loading: true})
  const [user, updateUser] = useState({})
  let didCancel = false
  useEffect(() => {
    getProducts()
    checkUser(updateUser)
    return () => didCancel = true
  }, [])
  async function getProducts() {
    const data = await API.get('ecommerceapi', '/products')
    console.log('data: ', data)
    if (didCancel) return
    setState({
      products: data.data.Items, loading: false
    })
  }
  async function deleteItem(id) {
    try {
      const products = state.products.filter(p => p.id !== id)
      setState({ ...state, products })
      await API.del('ecommerceapi', '/products', { body: { id } })
      console.log('successfully deleted item')
    } catch (err) {
      console.log('error: ', err)
    }
  }
  return (
    <Container>
      <List
        itemLayout="horizontal"
        dataSource={state.products}
        loading={state.loading}
        renderItem={item => (
          <List.Item
            actions={user.isAuthorized ?
              [<p onClick={() => deleteItem(item.id)}
              key={item.id}>delete</p>] : null}
          >
            <List.Item.Meta
              title={item.name}
              description={item.price}
```

```
            />
          </List.Item>
        )}
      />
    </Container>
  )
}

export default Main
```

Testing It Out

Now, we should be able to run the app and test it out:

```
~ npm start
```

Summary

Congratulations, you've now successfully deployed a full stack serverless CRUD+ List app.

Here are a few things to keep in mind from this chapter:

- Lambda functions can be invoked from many different event types, including API calls, image uploads, database operations, and authentication events. In this chapter, we've enabled `Function` invocations from both HTTP events as well as authentication events.

- Running an Express server in a Lambda function is a great way to extend the functionality of a single function.

- The `API` category takes in two required arguments when working with REST APIs: the API name and the path. It also takes in an optional third argument, an object that can contain any arguments you may want to send in a POST request.

- When interacting with DynamoDB from a Node.js Lambda function, use the DynamoDB document client, as it offers an easy-to-use API for creating, updating, deleting, and querying items from a DynamoDB database.

## CHAPTER 8

AWS AppSync In-Depth

In Chapter 3, we learned about GraphQL and created a basic GraphQL API. In this chapter, we'll expand upon these concepts to create a music festival app using AWS AppSync (*https://github.com/dabit3/full-stack-serverless-code/tree/master/appsync-in-depth*), from this book's GitHub repo.

This app will require the following:

- Amazon DynamoDB tables will be used for shows and stages.
- GraphQL API will be used for creating, reading, updating, deleting, and listing shows and stages.
- Only admins should be able to create, update, or delete a show or a stage.
- All users should be able to view shows and stages.
- Relationships should be enabled between shows and stages.
- Users should be able to view all shows as well as navigate to view show details.

Building Skills for GraphQL, AppSync API, and React Router

In this section, we'll cover how to model relationships between GraphQL types, how to implement authorization rules on GraphQL types and fields, how to enable multiple authorization modes for an AppSync API, and how to enable route parameters using React Router.

First we'll briefly cover each of these topics, and when we start building out the app, we will get into them in greater depth.

Relationships Between GraphQL Types

When creating a GraphQL API, or any API, modeling relationships between data becomes very important to understand. For example, the app that we are building will have the following two types:

Stage
> This type will hold the stage information for individual performances, including the stage name and stage ID. Each stage will have a number of performances that are associated with it.

Performance
> This type will hold the individual performance information, including the performer, the description, the stage of the performance, and the time of the performance.

For this type of API, ideally you would want to have at least the following access patterns:

- Query for a single stage and performances for the stage
- Query for all stages and performances for each stage
- Query for an individual performance and the corresponding stage info
- Query for all performances and the corresponding stage info

The question is now usually this: how can you enable these different relationships and access patterns? And in our case, how can we do this using a NoSQL database like DynamoDB? There are two ways to accomplish this:

- Pattern your data in DynamoDB in a way that enables all of these access patterns to be performed using a single table by taking advantage of a combination of primary keys, sort keys, and local secondary indexes. For this to work with AppSync, we would have to write and maintain all of the resolver logic by hand and from scratch.
- Enable these relationships directly at the resolver level. Because we are using GraphQL, and GraphQL enables per-field resolvers, this can be done. To understand this better let's take a look at one of the types we will be working with.

Stage type in GraphQL

To better understand these concepts, let's take a look at one of the types we will be working with:

```
type Stage {
  id: ID!
  name: String!
  performances: [Performance]
}
```

When creating a resolver, or resolvers, for this type, here is an example chain of actions that you could assume would happen when a request is made for stages and corresponding performances:

1. The main `Stage` GraphQL resolver will use the stage ID to retrieve the stage information from the Stage table in the database.

2. The field of `performances` on the `Stage` type will have its own GraphQL resolver. This resolver should use the stage ID to retrieve the related performances by querying the database using a GSI, returning only the performances for that *stage* ID.

GraphQL Transform: @connection

In Chapter 3, we used the `@model` directive of the GraphQL Transform library to scaffold out an entire backend, including resolvers, databases, and additional GraphQL schema. As a recap, the GraphQL Transform is a library of directives that allow us to "decorate" a GraphQL schema and add additional functionality.

Here, we'll be introducing a couple of new directives, including `@connection`, which enables us to model these relationships and generate the necessary resolvers with only a few lines of code.

Multiple Authentication Types

In Chapter 3, we created a GraphQL API using the API key as the authentication type. This is fine for certain circumstances, like when you want to have a GraphQL query available to all users of your app.

AppSync supports four main authentication methods:

The API key
> The API key requires that, when making an HTTP request, you send the API key in the header in the form of `x-api-key` in some form or fashion. If you are using the Amplify client as we have done so far in this book, then this is automatically sent for you.

Amazon Cognito user pools

> Amazon Cognito, the managed authentication service we've used throughout this book, is one of the mechanisms we will be using in this chapter. Using Amazon Cognito, we can configure private and group access to the API itself and to GraphQL types and fields.

OpenID Connect

> OpenID Connect enables you to bring your own authentication provider, so if you prefer another authentication service like Auth0, or your company has its own authentication implementation, you can still use it to authenticate against an AppSync API.

IAM

> AWS IAM type enforces the AWS Signature Version 4 signing process on the GraphQL API. You can use an AWS IAM UnAuthenticated Role from Cognito identity pools for public access, allowing a more secure way to enable public access against your AppSync API versus an API key.

Here we will use a combination of the API key and Amazon Cognito to provide multiple authentication types for the API, enabling public read access and private read and write access.

Authorization

Using the GraphQL Transform library, we can also define different authorization rules for the API by using the `@auth` directive.

Using `@auth`, we can define different types of rules, including (but not limited to) the following:

- Enable all users to create and read, but only the owner of the created item to update and delete.
- Enable only users of a certain group to be able to create, update, or delete.
- Enable all users to read, but not perform any other actions.
- A combination of the preceding rules.

In this instance, the app we will be building will support both private and public access, but we will need to also enable more control over these rules. We need to support the following:

- Authenticated users who are part of the Amazon Cognito group named Admin will be able to perform all actions: create, read, update, and delete.
- Users who are not authenticated will have access, but will only be able to read.

Custom Data Access Patterns Using GSIs

One of the most powerful things about DynamoDB is that it allows (at the time of this writing) 20 additional GSIs per table. Using either a GSI or a combination of GSI + sort key (also think of this as a filter key), you are able to create extremely flexible and powerful data access patterns for your data. The GraphQL Transform library also has a directive, @key, that makes it simple to configure custom index structures for @model types.

We'll use the @key directive to create an access pattern that will allow us to query performances for a given stage ID by setting the stage ID as the GSI on the Performance table. Doing this will allow us to be able to request stages and their corresponding performances in a single GraphQL query.

That completes our skills overview; let's get started building the app.

Starting to Build the App

To get started, we'll again be walking through the steps of creating a new React project, installing dependencies, initializing a new Amplify app, and adding features via the CLI.

Change into the directory where you would like the app to live, and create a new React project:

```
~ npx create-react-app festivalapp
~ cd festivalapp
```

Next, install the dependencies:

```
~ npm install aws-amplify antd @aws-amplify/ui-react react-router-dom
```

Creating the Amplify App and Adding the Features

Next, initialize a new Amplify project in the root of the project directory:

```
~ amplify init

# Follow the steps to give the project a name, environment name, and set the
  default text editor.
# Accept defaults for everything else and choose your AWS Profile.
```

Now, the Amplify project has been initialized and we can go ahead and start adding features.

Building the Backend

The first feature we will add is authentication. This app will need to have basic authentication but will also need to have the ability to add admin users dynamically via a Lambda post-confirmation trigger like we did in Chapter 6. To enable this, we will create the authentication service as well as a Lambda trigger that will allow us to add a predefined set of users into an Admin group as they sign up.

Authentication

To add authentication with Cognito, we'll again use the `auth` category:

```
~ amplify add auth

? Do you want to use the default authentication and security configuration?
  Default configuration
? How do you want users to be able to sign in? Username
? Do you want to configure advanced settings? Yes
? What attributes are required for signing up? Email
? Do you want to enable any of the following capabilities? Add User to Group
? Enter the name of the group to which users will be added. Admin
? Do you want to edit your add-to-group function now? Y
```

Update the function with the following code and configure the `adminEmails` array:

```
// amplify/backend/function/<function_name>/src/add-to-group.js

const aws = require('aws-sdk');

exports.handler = async (event, context, callback) => {
  const cognitoProvider = new
  aws.CognitoIdentityServiceProvider({
    apiVersion: '2016-04-18'
  });

  let isAdmin = false
  /* set your admin emails here */
  const adminEmails = ['user1@somedomain.com', 'user2@somedomain.com']

  // If the user is one of the admins, set the isAdmin variable to true
  if (adminEmails.indexOf(event.request.userAttributes.email) !== -1) {
    isAdmin = true
  }

  const groupParams = {
    UserPoolId: event.userPoolId,
  }

  const userParams = {
    UserPoolId: event.userPoolId,
    Username: event.userName,
```

```
  }

  if (isAdmin) {
    groupParams.GroupName = 'Admin',
    userParams.GroupName = 'Admin'

    // First check to see if the groups exists, and if not create the group
    try {
      await cognitoProvider.getGroup(groupParams).promise();
    } catch (e) {
      await cognitoProvider.createGroup(groupParams).promise();
    }

    // If the user is an administrator, place them in the Admin group
    try {
      await cognitoProvider.adminAddUserToGroup(userParams).promise();
      callback(null, event);
    } catch (e) {
      callback(e);
    }
  } else {
    // If the user is in neither group, proceed with no action
    callback(null, event)
  }
}
```

Now, the authentication service has been set up and we can continue on to the next step: creating the AppSync API.

The AppSync API

Next, we'll create the AppSync GraphQL API. Remember that for this API, we will need to enable multiple authentication types for both public and protected access. This can all be enabled by the CLI.

To add the AppSync API, we'll use the api category:

```
~ amplify add api

? Please select from one of the below mentioned services: GraphQL
? Provide API name: festivalapi
? Choose an authorization type for the API: Amazon Cognito User Pool
Do you want to configure advanced settings for the GraphQL API: Yes
? Configure additional auth types? Y
? Choose the additional authorization types you want to configure for the API:
  API key
? Enter a description for the API key: public (or a custom description)
? After how many days from now the API key should expire: 365 (or a custom
  expiration date)
? Configure conflict detection? N
? Do you have an annotated GraphQL schema? N
? Do you want a guided schema creation? Y
```

```
? What best describes your project: Single object with fields
? Do you want to edit the schema now? Y
```

This should open the GraphQL schema, located at *amplify/backend/api/festivalapi/schema.graphql*, in your text editor.

The schema we will be using has two main types, a `Stage` and a `Performance`. Use the following schema and continue (we will walk through how it works in the next step):

```
type Stage @model
  @auth(rules: [
  { allow: public, operations: [read] },
  { allow: groups, groups: ["Admin"] }
]) {
  id: ID!
  name: String!
  performances: [Performance] @connection(keyName: "byStageId", fields: ["id"])
}

type Performance @model
  @key(name: "byStageId", fields: ["performanceStageId"])
  @auth(rules: [
  { allow: public, operations: [read] },
  { allow: groups, groups: ["Admin"] }
]) {
  id: ID!
  performanceStageId: ID!
  productID: ID
  performer: String!
  imageUrl: String
  description: String!
  time: String
  stage: Stage @connection
}
```

Let's look at the directives we used and how they work.

@auth

First, the `@auth` directive allows us to pass in an array of authorization rules. Each rule has an `allow` field (required) as well as other metadata (optional), including things like specifying the provider if it is different than the default authorization type.

In the `Stage` and `Performance` type, we've used two authorization types, one for group access (`groups`) and another for public access (`public`). You'll notice that for the public access, we've also set an array of operations. This array should contain a list of the operations we would like to enable on the API. If there are no operations listed, then by default all operations would be enabled.

@key

The `@key` directive enables us to add GSIs and sort keys to a DynamoDB table for custom data access patterns. In the preceding schema, we've created a key called `byStageId` that will allow us to query the Performance table for performances by stage ID using a field called `performanceStageId` (on the `Performance` table). The resolver for the `performances` field will then use the ID of the stage to query for performances by stage ID.

@connection

The `@connection` directive allows us to model relationships between types. Types of relationships that can be created are belongs to, one to many, many to one, or many to many. In this example, we've created two relationships:

- A relationship between a stage and a performance (one stage has many performances)
- A relationship between a performance and a stage (a performance belongs to a stage)

Deploying the Services

With all of the services configured, we're ready to deploy the backend:

```
~ amplify push
```

The services have been deployed and we can begin writing the client code.

Building the Frontend

Now that the project has been created and configured and the backend has been deployed, we can start setting up the client!

The first thing we will do is create the files we will need for this app:

```
~ cd src
~ touch Container.js Footer.js Nav.js Admin.js Router.js Performance.js Home.js
```

The next thing we will need to do is open *src/index.js* to add the Amplify configuration, import the Ant Design styles, and replace the main component with the Router that we will be creating soon. Update the file with the following code:

```
/* src/index.js */
import React from 'react';
import ReactDOM from 'react-dom';
import Router from './Router';
import 'antd/dist/antd.css';
```

```
import Amplify from 'aws-amplify'
import config from './aws-exports'
Amplify.configure(config)

ReactDOM.render(<Router />, document.getElementById('root'));
```

Container

Now, let's create the Container component that will serve as a reusable component to add padding and styling for our views:

```
/* src/Container.js */
import React from 'react'

export default function Container({ children }) {
  return (
    <div style={container}>
      {children}
    </div>
  )
}

const container = {
  padding: '30px 40px',
  minHeight: 'calc(100vh - 120px)'
}
```

Footer

Here, we'll create the Footer component that will serve as a reusable component to add a basic footer, as well as a link for admins to be able to sign up and sign in:

```
/* src/Footer.js */
import React from 'react'
import { Link } from 'react-router-dom'

function Footer() {
  return (
    <div style={footerStyle}>
      <Link to="/admin">
        Admins
      </Link>
    </div>
  )
}

const footerStyle = {
  borderTop: '1px solid #ddd',
  display: 'flex',
  alignItems: 'center',
  padding: 20
}
```

```
export default Footer
```

Nav

Now, open *src/Nav.js* to create the basic navigation. There will only be one link: a link back to the main view that will hold all of the shows and performances:

```
/* src/Nav.js */
import React from 'react'
import { Link } from 'react-router-dom'
import { Menu } from 'antd'
import { HomeOutlined } from '@ant-design/icons'

const Nav = (props) => {
  const { current } = props
  return (
    <div>
      <Menu selectedKeys={[current]} mode="horizontal">
        <Menu.Item key='home'>
          <Link to={`/`}>
            <HomeOutlined />Home
          </Link>
        </Menu.Item>
      </Menu>
    </div>
  )
}

export default Nav
```

Admin

The Admin component we'll create will only do three things for now: allow a user to sign up, sign in, and sign out. The idea for this component is to give admins a way to sign up so they can then create and manage the API as an admin.

 Remember, when someone signs up, if their email is enabled in the Lambda trigger, they will be placed in the Admin group after signing up. They will then be able to perform mutations to create, update, and delete stages and performances.

If you ever need to update your backend code like the GraphQL schema or Lambda function, you can make the changes locally, then run amplify push to deploy the changes to the backend:

```
/* src/Admin.js */
import React from 'react'
import { withAuthenticator, AmplifySignOut } from '@aws-amplify/ui-react'
```

```
import { Auth } from 'aws-amplify'
import { Button } from 'antd'

function Admin() {
  return (
    <div>
      <h1 style={titleStyle}>Admin</h1>
      <AmplifySignOut />
    </div>
  )
}

const titleStyle = {
  fontWeight: 'normal',
  margin: '0px 0px 10px 0px'
}

export default withAuthenticator(Admin)
```

Router

Now let's create the Router:

```
/* src/Router.js */
import React, { useState, useEffect } from 'react'
import { HashRouter, Switch, Route } from 'react-router-dom'

import Home from './Home'
import Admin from './Admin'
import Nav from './Nav'
import Footer from './Footer'
import Container from './Container'
import Performance from './Performance'

const Router = () => {
  const [current, setCurrent] = useState('home')
  useEffect(() => {
    setRoute()
    window.addEventListener('hashchange', setRoute)
    return () => window.removeEventListener('hashchange', setRoute)
  }, [])
  function setRoute() {
    const location = window.location.href.split('/')
    const pathname = location[location.length-1]
    setCurrent(pathname ? pathname : 'home')
  }
  return (
    <HashRouter>
      <Nav current={current} />
      <Container>
        <Switch>
          <Route exact path="/" component={Home}/>
```

```
        <Route exact path="/performance/:id" component={Performance} />
        <Route exact path="/admin" component={Admin}/>
      </Switch>
    </Container>
    <Footer />
  </HashRouter>
)
}

export default Router
```

In this component, we combine the router with the persistent UI components like the Container and Footer.

The app has three routes:

Home
> This is the main route that will render the stages and performances.

Performance
> This is this is the route that will render an individual performance and details around the performance.

Admin
> This is the route that will render the sign-up/sign-in page for admins.

In the Performance route, you will see that we are using a path that looks like this:

```
/performance/:id
```

Doing this allows us to have URL parameters, so if we hit a route like this, we will be able to easily extract the ID from the URL:

```
/performance/100
```

Hitting a route with URL parameters will allow us to access them in the component itself. This is useful because we will be using the ID of the performance to fetch the performance details, and having them easily accessible in the route parameters enables this. It also enables you to easily build apps that support deep linking.

Performance

Next, let's create the Performance component:

```
/* src/Performance.js */
import React, { useState, useEffect } from 'react'
import { useParams } from 'react-router-dom'
import { getPerformance } from './graphql/queries'
import { API } from 'aws-amplify'

function Performance() {
  const [performance, setPerformance] = useState(null)
```

```
const [loading, setLoading] = useState(true)

let { id } = useParams()
useEffect(() => {
  fetchPerformanceInfo()
}, [])
async function fetchPerformanceInfo() {
  try {
    const talkInfo = await API.graphql({
      query: getPerformance,
      variables: { id },
      authMode: 'API_KEY'
    })
    setPerformance(talkInfo.data.getPerformance)
    setLoading(false)
  } catch (err) {
    console.log('error fetching talk info...', err)
    setLoading(false)
  }
}

return (
  <div>
    <p>Performance</p>
    { loading && <h3>Loading...</h3>}
    {
      performance && (
        <div>
          <h1>{performance.performer}</h1>
          <h3>{performance.time}</h3>
          <p>{performance.description}</p>
        </div>
      )
    }
  </div>
)
}

export default Performance
```

The render method of this component is pretty basic; it's just rendering the performance `performer`, `time`, and `description`. What is interesting about this component is how we get that information. We do so with the following flow:

1. We create two pieces of state using the `useState` hook: `loading` (set to true) and `performance` (set to null). We also create a variable called `id` that uses the `usePar ams` helper from React Router to get the route parameter of `id`.

2. When the component loads, we use the `useEffect` hook to immediately call the `fetchPerformanceInfo` function.

3. The `fetchPerformanceInfo` function will use the `id` from the route params to call the AppSync API. The API call here uses `API.graphql`, passing in the `variables`, `query`, and the `authMode`. By default, our API is using Cognito User Pools as the auth mode. Any time we would like to override this, like in this case to make a public API call, we need to specify the `authMode` in the API call itself.

4. Once the data is returned from the API, we call `setLoading` and `setPerformance` to update the UI and render the data coming back from the API.

Home

Now, let's create the last component, the `Home` component:

```
/* src/Home.js */
import React, { useEffect, useState } from 'react'
import { API } from 'aws-amplify'
import { listStages } from './graphql/queries'
import { Link } from 'react-router-dom'
import { List } from 'antd';

function Home() {
  const [stages, setStages] = useState([])
  const [loading, setLoading] = useState(true)
  useEffect(() => {
    getStages()
  }, [])
  async function getStages() {
    const apiData = await API.graphql({
      query: listStages,
      authMode: 'API_KEY'
    })
    const { data: { listStages: { items }}} = apiData
    setLoading(false)
    setStages(items)
  }

  return (
    <div>
      <h1 style={heading}>Stages</h1>
        { loading && <h2>Loading...</h2>}
        {
          stages.map(stage => (
            <div key={stage.id} style={stageInfo}>
              <p style={infoHeading}>{stage.name}</p>
              <p style={infoTitle}>Performances</p>
              <List
                itemLayout="horizontal"
                dataSource={stage.performances.items}
                renderItem={performance => (
                  <List.Item>
                    <List.Item.Meta
```

```
                      title={<Link style={performerInfo}
                      to={`/performance/${
                            performance.id}`}>{
                            performance.performer}</Link>
                      }
                      description={performance.time}
                    />
                  </List.Item>
                )}
              />
            </div>
          ))
        }
      </div>
    )
  }
}

const heading = { fontSize: 44, fontWeight: 300, marginBottom: 5 }
const stageInfo = { padding: '20px 0px 10px', borderBottom: '2px solid #ddd' }
const infoTitle = { fontWeight: 'bold' , fontSize: 18 }
const infoHeading = { fontSize: 30, marginBottom: 5 }
const performerInfo = { fontSize: 24 }

export default Home
```

The logic in this component is actually very similar to what we did in the
Performance component:

1. Create two main pieces of state using the useState hook: stages (set to an empty
   array), and loading (set to true).

2. When the app loads, we use the API class with a custom authMode of API_KEY to
   call the AppSync API.

3. When the data comes back from the API, set the state for the stages and set loading to false.

Now, the app is finished, but there's just one more thing. Because we have created a
custom access pattern for the performances resolver, we need to update the list
Stages query definition to also return the performances. To do this, update the list
Stages query with the following:

```
/* src/graphql/queries.js */

export const listStages = /* GraphQL */ `
  query ListStages(
    $filter: ModelStageFilterInput
    $nextToken: String
  ) {
    listStages(filter: $filter, limit: 500, nextToken: $nextToken) {
      items {
```

```
          id
          name
          performances {
            items {
              id
              time
              performer
              description
            }
          }
        }
        nextToken
      }
    }
`;
```

Now, the app is completed and we can populate some data. Start the app and sign up with an admin user:

```
~ npm start
```

Click the Admins link in the footer to sign up. Once you've signed up, open the AppSync console:

```
~ amplify console api
```

```
> Choose GraphQL
```

In the Queries panel of the console, you will need to click Login with User Pools to sign in using the username and password of the user you just created. When prompted for the ClientID, use the aws_user_pools_web_client_id located in the *aws-exports.js* file of your local project.

Next, create at least one stage and one performance.

```
mutation createStage {
  createStage(input: {
    id: "stage-1"
    name: "Stage 1"
  }) {
    id name
  }
}

mutation createPerformance {
  createPerformance(input: {
    performanceStageId: "stage-1"
    performer: "Dreek"
    description: "Dreek LIVE in NYC! Don't miss out, performing
                  all of the hits with a few surprise performances!"
    time: "Monday, May 4 2022"
  }) {
    id performer description
```

```
    }
}
```

Now, our database has some data, and we should be able to view it in our app and navigate between the main view and the detail view for each performance!

Summary

Here are a few things to keep in mind from this chapter:

- The GraphQL Transform directive enables you to add powerful features to your GraphQL API like authorization rules, relationships, and custom indexes for additional data access patterns.

- The @auth directive allows you to pass in an array of rules to define authorization rules on types and fields.

- The @connection directive enables you to model relationships between GraphQL types.

- The @key directive enables you to define custom indexes for custom data access patterns and to enhance existing relationships.

- When creating an API with multiple authorization types, you will have a Primary authorization type that will be the default when making API calls. Whenever you need to override the Primary authorization type, you must pass in the authMode parameter to the API class defining the authorization type you would like to use.

## CHAPTER 9

Building Offline Apps with Amplify DataStore

So far in this book, we've worked with REST APIs and GraphQL APIs. When working with the GraphQL APIs, we used the API class to directly call mutations and queries against the API.

Amplify also supports another type of API for interacting with AppSync: Amplify DataStore. DataStore has a different approach than a traditional GraphQL API.

Instead of interacting with the GraphQL API itself, using queries and mutations, DataStore introduces a client-side SDK that allows you to write to and read from a local store and persists this data locally using the local storage engine of the platform you are working with (i.e., IndexDB for web and SQLite for native iOS and Android). DataStore then automatically syncs the local data to the GraphQL backend for you as updates are made both locally and remotely.

Using the DataStore SDK, you then only have to perform the operations like save, update, and delete, writing directly to DataStore itself. DataStore handles everything else for you: it syncs your data to the cloud when you have an internet connection, and if you're not online, will queue it for the next time you're connected.

DataStore also handles conflict detection and resolution for you with one of three built-in conflict-resolution strategies:

AutoMerge
> GraphQL type information on an object is inspected at runtime to perform merge operations (suggested option).

Optimistic concurrency
> The latest written item to your database will be used with a version check against the incoming record.

Custom
> Use a Lambda function and write any custom business logic you wish to the process when merging or rejecting updates.

About Amplify DataStore

Amplify DataStore (*https://oreil.ly/Wv_TT*) is a combination of the following things:

- AppSync GraphQL API
- Local storage repository and syncing engine that also persists data offline
- Client-side SDK for interacting with the local storage repository
- Special sync-enabled GraphQL resolvers (generated by the Amplify CLI) that enable sophisticated conflict detection and conflict resolution on the server

Amplify DataStore Overview

When getting started with DataStore, you still create the API as we have done in past chapters. The main difference is, when creating the API, you will enable *conflict detection* in the advanced settings of the CLI flow.

From there, to enable DataStore on the client, we need to create models for DataStore to use to interact with the storage repository. This can easily be done by just using the GraphQL schema you already have and running a build command—`amplify code gen models`—from the CLI.

Now, you are all set up and can begin interacting with DataStore.

Amplify DataStore Operations

To interact with the Store, first import the `DataStore` API from Amplify and the Model you'd like to use. From there, you can perform actions against the store.

See Table 9-1 for some available operations.

Table 9-1. Amplify DataStore Operations

Operation	Commands
Import the model and DataStore API	```import { DataStore } from '@aws-amplify/datastore'``` ```import { Message} from './models'```

Saving data	```await DataStore.save(```
	 ``` new Message({```
	 ``` title: 'Hello World',```
	 ``` sender: 'Chris'```
	 ``` })```
	 ```))```

Reading data	```const posts = await DataStore.query(Post)```
Deleting data	```const message = await DataStore.query(Message, '123')``` ```DataStore.delete(message)```

Updating data	```const message = await DataStore.query(Message, '123')```
	 ```await DataStore.save(```
	 ``` Post.copyOf(message, updated => {```
	 ``` updated.title = 'My new title'```
	 ``` })```
	 ```)```

Observing/subscribing to changes in data for real-time functionality	```const subscription = DataStore.observe(Message).sub```
	 ```scribe(msg => {```
	 ``` console.log(message.model, message.opType, message.element)```
	 ```});```

DataStore Predicates

You can apply predicate filters against the DataStore using the fields defined on your GraphQL type along with the following conditions supported by DynamoDB:

```
Strings: eq | ne | le | lt | ge | gt | contains | notContains | beginsWith
         | between
Numbers: eq | ne | le | lt | ge | gt | between
Lists: contains | notContains
```

For example, if you wanted a list of all messages that have a title that includes "Hello":

```
const messages = await DataStore
  .query(Message, m =>
m.title('contains', 'Hello'))
```

You can also chain multiple predicates into a single operation:

```
const message = await DataStore
  .query(Message, m => m.title('contains', 'Hello').sender('eq', 'Chris'))
```

These predicates enable you to have many ways to retrieve different selection sets from your local data. Instead of retrieving the entire collection and filtering on the client, you are able to query from the store exactly the data that you need.

Building an Offline and Real-Time App with Amplify DataStore

The app that we will build is a real-time and offline-first message board, as shown in Figure 9-1.

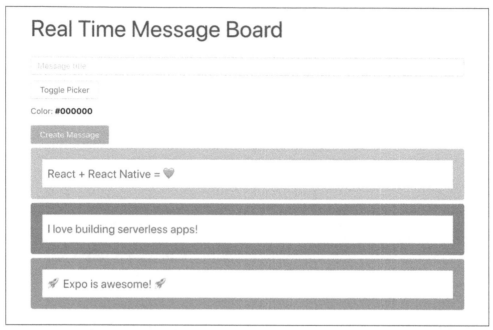

Figure 9-1. Real-time message board

Users of the app can create a new message and all other users will receive the message in real time. If a user goes offline, they will continue to be able to create messages. Once they are online, the messages will be synced with the backend, and all other messages created by other users will also be fetched and synced locally.

Our app will perform three types of operations against the DataStore API:

save
> Creating a new item in the DataStore; saves the item locally and performs a GraphQL mutation behind the scenes.

query
> Reading from the DataStore; returns a single item or list (array) and performs a GraphQL query behind the scenes.

observe
> Listening for changes (create, update, delete) in data and performs a GraphQL subscription behind the scenes.

Let's get started.

Creating the Base Project

To get started, we will create a new React project, initialize an Amplify app, and install the dependencies.

The first thing we will do is create the React project:

```
~ npx create-react-app rtmessageboard
~ cd rtmessageboard
```

Next, we will install the local dependencies.

Amplify supports a full installation of Amplify, and *scoped* (modular) installations for specific APIs. Scoped packages reduce the bundle size, since we're installing only the code that we are using. Since we are only using the DataStore API, we can install the scoped DataStore package.

We will also install Ant Design (antd) for styling, React Color (react-color) for an easy-to-use color picker, and the scoped dependency for Amplify Core in order to still configure the Amplify app with *aws-exports.js*:

```
~ npm install @aws-amplify/core @aws-amplify/datastore antd react-color
```

Next, initialize a new Amplify project:

```
~ amplify init

# Follow the steps to give the project a name, environment name, and set the
  default text editor.
# Accept defaults for everything else and choose your AWS Profile.
```

Creating the API

Now we will create the AppSync GraphQL API:

```
~ amplify add api

? Please select from one of the below mentioned services: GraphQL
? Provide API name: rtmessageboard
? Choose the default authorization type for the API: API key
? Enter a description for the API key: public
? After how many days from now the API key should expire (1-365): 365 (or your
  preferred expiration)
? Do you want to configure advanced settings for the GraphQL API: Yes
? Configure additional auth types: N
? Configure conflict detection: Y
```

```
? Select the default resolution strategy: Auto Merge
? Do you have an annotated GraphQL schema: N
? Do you want a guided schema creation: Y
? What best describes your project: Single object with fields
? Do you want to edit the schema now: Y
```

Update the schema with the following type:

```
type Message @model {
  id: ID!
  title: String!
  color: String
  image: String
  createdAt: String
}
```

Now that we have created the GraphQL API, and we have a GraphQL schema to work with, we can create the models we'll need for working the local DataStore API (based on the GraphQL schema):

```
~ amplify codegen models
```

This will create a new folder in our project called *models*. Using the models in this folder, we can start interacting with the DataStore API. Deploy the API:

```
~ amplify push --y
```

With the backend deployed, we can start writing the client-side code.

Writing the Client-Side Code

First, open *src/index.js* and configure the Amplify app by adding the following code below the last import:

```
import 'antd/dist/antd.css'
import Amplify from '@aws-amplify/core'
import config from './aws-exports'
Amplify.configure(config)
```

Notice that we are importing from `@aws-amplify/core` instead of `aws-amplify`.

Next, open *App.js* and update it with the following code:

```
/* src/App.js */
import React, { useState, useEffect } from 'react'
import { SketchPicker } from 'react-color'
import { Input, Button } from 'antd'
import { DataStore } from '@aws-amplify/datastore'
import { Message} from './models'

const initialState = { color: '#000000', title: '' }
function App() {
  const [formState, updateFormState] = useState(initialState)
  const [messages, updateMessages] = useState([])
```

```
const [showPicker, updateShowPicker] = useState(false)
useEffect(() => {
  fetchMessages()
  const subscription = DataStore
    .observe(Message)
    .subscribe(() => fetchMessages())
  return () => subscription.unsubscribe()
}, [])
async function fetchMessages() {
  const messages = await DataStore.query(Message)
  updateMessages(messages)
}
function onChange(e) {
  if (e.hex) {
    updateFormState({ ...formState, color: e.hex})
  } else { updateFormState({ ...formState, [e.target.name]: e.target.value}) }
}
async function createMessage() {
  if (!formState.title) return
  await DataStore.save(new Message({ ...formState }))
  updateFormState(initialState)
}
return (
  <div style={container}>
    <h1 style={heading}>Real Time Message Board</h1>
    <Input
      onChange={onChange}
      name="title"
      placeholder="Message title"
      value={formState.title}
      style={input}
    />
    <div>
      <Button
      onClick={() => updateShowPicker(!showPicker)}
      style={button}
      >Toggle Color Picker</Button>
      <p>Color:
        <span
         style={{fontWeight: 'bold', color: formState.color}}>{formState.color}
        </span>
      </p>
    </div>
    {
      showPicker && (
        <SketchPicker
         color={formState.color}
         onChange={onChange} /
        >
      )
    }
    <Button type="primary" onClick={createMessage}>Create Message</Button>
```

```
      {
        messages.map(message => (
          <div
            key={message.id}
            style={{...messageStyle, backgroundColor: message.color}}
          >
            <div style={messageBg}>
              <p style={messageTitle}>{message.title}</p>
            </div>
          </div>
        ))
      }
    </div>
  );
}

const container = { width: '100%', padding: 40, maxWidth: 900 }
const input = { marginBottom: 10 }
const button = { marginBottom: 10 }
const heading = { fontWeight: 'normal', fontSize: 40 }
const messageBg = { backgroundColor: 'white' }
const messageStyle = { padding: '20px', marginTop: 7, borderRadius: 4 }
const messageTitle = { margin: 0, padding: 9, fontSize: 20  }

export default App
```

Let's walk through the most important parts of what's going on in this component:

1. We import the `DataStore` API from Amplify as well as the `Message` model.

2. We create three pieces of component state using the `useState` hook:

   formState
   : This object manages the state for the form, including the `title` and `color` that will be used to display the background color of the message.

   messages
   : This will manage the array of messages once they are fetched from DataStore.

   showPicker
   : This will manage a Boolean value that will be toggled to show and hide a color picker to fill the `color` value for the message (by default, the color is set to black and held in the `formState`).

3. When the component loads (in `useEffect`), we fetch all messages by invoking the `fetchMessages` function and create a subscription (`DataStore.observe`) to listen to message updates. When a subscription is fired, we again invoke the `fetchMessages` function because we know there has been an update and we

would like to update the app with the most recent data coming back from the API.

4. The `fetchMessages` function calls `DataStore.query` and then updates the component state with the returned array of messages.

5. The `onChange` handler handles the updates to the form input as well as the color picker being changed.

6. In `createMessage`, we first check to make sure the title field is populated. If it is, we save the message using `DataStore.save` and then reset the form state.

Let's test it out:

```
~ npm start
```

Testing the Offline Functionality

Try going offline, creating a new mutation, and then coming back online. You should notice that, when back online, the app takes all of the messages created when you were offline and creates them in the database.

To verify this, open the AppSync API in the AWS Console:

```
~ amplify console api
? Please select from one of the below mentioned services: GraphQL
```

Next, click Data Sources and then open the Message Table resource. You should now see the items in the Message Table.

Testing the Real-Time Functionality

To test out the real-time functionality, open another browser window so that you have two windows running the same app. Then create a new item in one window and see the update come through automatically in the other window.

Summary

Here are a few things to keep in mind from this chapter:

- Amplify enables two different APIs to interact with AppSync: the `API` category as well as DataStore.

- When using DataStore, you are no longer sending HTTP requests directly to the API. Instead, you are writing to the local storage engine, and DataStore then takes care of syncing to and from the cloud.

- Amplify DataStore works offline by default.

## CHAPTER 10

Working with Images and Storage

Many applications need to have a way to manage file, image, and video storage. While it's possible to transform these objects into binary data and store them directly in your database, it's usually better not to. Instead, using a managed file-hosting service like Amazon S3 is better because it's less expensive, faster, and just as secure.

In this chapter, we'll look at how to create a photo-sharing app that renders posts with photos in a stream in real time, allowing you to share an image along with a caption for the image.

Using Amazon S3

Amazon S3 allows you to have secure file hosting that scales as you need it. Amplify uses S3 as the Storage category for handling the storage of files like images, videos, PDFs, and more.

When working with S3, you typically will have three types of file access available:

Public
> Items stored with public access will be accessible by all users of your app. These files are stored under the *public/* path in your S3 bucket. Public does not mean that anyone with the URL of the resource can view it, though. In order to be viewed, you must use the Amplify SDK to retrieve a temporarily signed URL of the resource. This signed URL will be set to expire after a set period of time (15 minutes by default).

Private
> Items are readable by all users, but writable only by the creating user. In S3, the files are stored under the path *private/{user_identity_id}*, where the *user_identity_id* corresponds to the unique Amazon Cognito ID for that user.

Protected

These files are only accessible for the individual user. Files are stored under the path *private/{user_identity_id}* where the *user_identity_id* corresponds to the unique Amazon Cognito ID for that user.

By default, when storing a file, it will be set to `public` unless otherwise specified:

```
await Storage.put('test.txt', 'Hello')
```

If you would like to specify either `private` or `protected` access, you need to specify the level when saving:

```
/* Private level access */
await Storage.put('test.txt', 'Private Content', {
  level: 'private',
  contentType: 'text/plain'
})

/* Protected level access */
await Storage.put('test.txt', 'Protected Content', {
  level: 'protected',
  contentType: 'text/plain'
})
```

The storage category uses Amazon S3 to store file types including images, PDFs, video, text files, and more.

To put this all together, we'll use a combination of a GraphQL API along with Amazon S3 to work as the backend for the app. The GraphQL schema will hold the fields for the image title, the image key stored in S3, and the unique ID.

Let's take a look at the schema we will be using:

```
type Post @model {
  id: ID!
  title: String!
  imageKey: String!
}
```

When creating a new post, there are two operations that will need to happen:

- The image is given a unique key and stored in the S3 bucket.
- The post metadata, including the image key, is stored in the GraphQL API.

When reading posts, this will be the sequence of events:

1. GraphQL query to read a list of posts from the GraphQL API.
2. Map over the posts array, getting a signed URL for each image in the list of posts.
3. Render the posts using the signed URL for the image as the image source.

The example we will build in this chapter implements a very common and useful pattern for building applications that rely on a combination of an API with references to large objects, such as images, videos, and files in general that are stored in S3.

Creating the Base Project

To get started, we will create a new React project, initialize an Amplify app, and install the dependencies.

The first thing we will do is create the React project:

```
~ npx create-react-app photo-app
~ cd photo-app
```

Next, we will install the local dependencies. This project will use Ant Design for styling (antd), the UUID package for creating unique identifiers (uuid) along with the AWS Amplify and AWS Amplify React packages:

```
~ npm install antd uuid aws-amplify @aws-amplify/ui-react
```

Next, initialize a new Amplify project:

```
~ amplify init

# Follow the steps to give the project a name, environment name, and set the
  default text editor.
# Accept defaults for everything else and choose your AWS Profile.
```

Adding Authentication

Next, add authentication using the auth category:

```
~ amplify add auth

? Do you want to use the default authentication and security configuration?
  Default configuration
? How do you want users to be able to sign in? Username
? Do you want to configure advanced settings? No, I am done.
```

Creating the API

Next, we will create the AppSync GraphQL API:

```
~ amplify add api

? Please select from one of the below mentioned services: GraphQL
? Provide API name: photoapp
? Choose an authorization type for the API: Amazon Cognito User Pool
? Do you want to configure advanced settings for the API? No
? Do you have an annotated GraphQL schema? N
? Do you want a guided schema creation? Y
```

```
? What best describes your project: Single object with fields
? Do you want to edit the schema now? Yes
```

For the GraphQL schema, use the following:

```
type Post @model {
  id: ID!
  title: String!
  imageKey: String!
}
```

Finally, we will add storage using the `storage` category:

```
~ amplify add storage

? Please select from one of the below mentioned services: Content
? Please provide a friendly name for your resource that will be used to label
  this category in the project: photos
? Please provide bucket name: <your_unique_bucket_name>
? Who should have access: Auth users only
? What kind of access do you want for Authenticated users? Choose all
  (create / update, read, & delete)
? Do you want to add a Lambda Trigger for your S3 Bucket? N
```

Now services have been configured and they are ready to be deployed:

```
~ amplify push
```

Now that the backend has been deployed, we can start writing the client-side code.

Writing the Client-Side Code

First, open *src/index.js* and configure the Amplify app by adding the following code below the last import:

```
import 'antd/dist/antd.css'
import Amplify from 'aws-amplify'
import config from './aws-exports'
Amplify.configure(config)
```

This app will have two views: one view for listing posts and one view for creating posts. Let's next create two new components for these views in the *src* directory:

```
~ cd src
~ touch Posts.js CreatePost.js
~ cd ..
```

Next, open *src/App.js* and update it with the following code:

```
/* src/App.js */
import React, { useState } from 'react';
import { Radio } from 'antd'
import { withAuthenticator, AmplifySignOut } from '@aws-amplify/ui-react'
import Posts from './Posts'
import CreatePost from './CreatePost'
```

```
function App() {
  const [viewState, updateViewState] = useState('viewPosts')

  return (
    <div style={container}>
      <h1>Photo App</h1>
      <Radio.Group
        value={viewState}
        onChange={e => updateViewState(e.target.value)}
      >
        <Radio.Button value="viewPosts">View Posts</Radio.Button>
        <Radio.Button value="addPost">Add Post</Radio.Button>
      </Radio.Group>
      {
        viewState === 'viewPosts' ? (
          <Posts />
        ) : (
          <CreatePost updateViewState={updateViewState} />
        )
      }
      <AmplifySignOut />
    </div>
  );
}

const container = { width: 500, margin: '0 auto', padding: 50 }

export default withAuthenticator(App);
```

This component imports the `Posts` and `CreatePost` components and renders one of them based on the `viewState` component state.

To create the `viewState`, we used the `useState` hook. To toggle the value of `view State`, we render a radio group from Ant Design that renders a button for either viewing posts (View Posts) or adding a new post (Add Post).

Next, open *src/CreatePost.js* and update it with the following code:

```
/* src/CreatePost.js */
import React, { useState } from 'react';
import { Button, Input } from 'antd'
import { v4 as uuid } from 'uuid'
import { createPost } from './graphql/mutations'
import { API, graphqlOperation, Storage } from 'aws-amplify'

const initialFormState = {
  title: '',
  image: {}
}

function CreatePost({ updateViewState }) {
```

```
    const [formState, updateFormState] = useState(initialFormState)

    function onChange(key, value) {
      updateFormState({ ...formState, [key]: value })
    }

    function setPhoto(e) {
      if (!e.target.files[0]) return
      const file = e.target.files[0]
      updateFormState({ ...formState, image: file })
    }

    async function savePhoto() {
      const { title, image } = formState
      if (!title || !image.name ) return

      const imageKey =
        uuid() + formState.image.name.replace(/\s/g, '-').toLowerCase()
      await Storage.put(imageKey, formState.image)
      const post = { title, imageKey }
      await API.graphql(graphqlOperation(createPost, { input: post }))
      updateViewState('viewPosts')
    }

    return (
      <div>
        <h2 style={heading}>Add Photo</h2>
        <Input
          onChange={e => onChange('title', e.target.value)}
          style={withMargin}
          placeholder="Title"
        />
        <input
          type='file'
          onChange={setPhoto}
          style={button}
        />
        <Button
          style={button}
          type="primary"
          onClick={savePhoto}
        >
        Save Photo</Button>
      </div>
    );
}

const heading = { margin: '20px 0px' }
const withMargin = { marginTop: 10 }
const button = { marginTop: 10 }

export default CreatePost
```

About this component

In this component, we allow users to upload an image and create a new post with the image and a title:

1. The state that this component holds is stored in the `formState` object, created using the `useState` hook. This object holds the post `title` as well as the post `image`.

2. `onChange` updates the `title` of the `formState` when the user types into the input.

3. `setPhoto` allows a user to upload an image and stores it in the `formState` as the `image`.

4. `savePhoto` is where we store the image in S3 and then save the post information to AppSync using a GraphQL mutation:

   a. We first create a variable called `imageKey` using a combination of the image `name` and a `uuid`.

   b. We then store the image in S3 using the `imageKey` as the reference.

   c. After the image is stored, we then make an API call to AppSync, creating a new `Post` using a GraphQL Mutation and passing in the post `title` and `image Key` as the fields.

Next, open *src/Posts.js* and update it with the following code:

```
/* src/Posts.js */
import React, { useReducer, useEffect } from 'react';
import { listPosts } from './graphql/queries'
import { onCreatePost } from './graphql/subscriptions'
import { API, graphqlOperation, Storage } from 'aws-amplify'

function reducer(state, action) {
  switch(action.type) {
    case 'SET_POSTS':
      return  action.posts
    case 'ADD_POST':
      return [action.post, ...state]
    default:
      return state
  }
}

async function getSignedPosts(posts) {
  const signedPosts = await Promise.all(
    posts.map(async item => {
      const signedUrl = await Storage.get(item.imageKey)
      item.imageUrl = signedUrl
      return item
    })
```

```
    )
    return signedPosts
}

function Posts() {
  const [posts, dispatch] = useReducer(reducer, [])

  useEffect(() => {
    fetchPosts()

    const subscription = API.graphql(graphqlOperation(onCreatePost)).subscribe({
      next: async post => {
        const newPost = post.value.data.onCreatePost
        const signedUrl = await Storage.get(newPost.imageKey)
        newPost.imageUrl = signedUrl
        dispatch({ type: 'ADD_POST', post: newPost })
      }
    })
    return () => subscription.unsubscribe()
  }, [])

  async function fetchPosts() {
    const postData = await API.graphql(graphqlOperation(listPosts))
    const { data: { listPosts: { items }}} = postData
    const signedPosts = await getSignedPosts(items)
    dispatch({ type: 'SET_POSTS', posts: signedPosts })
  }

  return (
    <div>
      <h2 style={heading}>Posts</h2>
      {
        posts.map(post => (
          <div key={post.id} style={postContainer}>
            <img style={postImage} src={post.imageUrl} />
            <h3 style={postTitle}>{post.title}</h3>
          </div>
        ))
      }
    </div>
  )
}

const postContainer = {
  padding: '20px 0px 0px',
  borderBottom: '1px solid #ddd'
}
const heading = { margin: '20px 0px' }
const postImage = { width: 400 }
const postTitle = { marginTop: 4 }

export default Posts
```

useReducer

In this component, we are using the `useReducer` hook to manage application state. We do this because we will be having a GraphQL subscription that will be handling data coming through in real time. Because `useState` creates a closure, we must move the state that is outside the component into a reducer.

The reducer has two actions, one for adding a single post (`ADD_POST`) and one for setting an array of posts (`SET_POSTS`).

About this component

There are two main things happening in this component:

`useEffect`

When the component loads, this hook will fire, creating a new GraphQL subscription and then calling the `fetchPosts` function that we will go over in the next step:

1. The subscription will listen for new posts that are created by using the `onCreatePost` subscription.

2. When a new post is created, the `next` function will fire and the data for the new post will come through in the function argument (`post`).

3. We then use the post image `imageKey` to get a signed URL by using the Storage API, calling `Storage.get`.

4. After getting the signed URL for the image, we add the `imageURL` field to the post and dipatch `ADD_POST` to add the new post to the state.

`fetchPosts`

This function fetches the posts from the API, then calls `getSignedPosts` passing in the posts:

1. The `getSignedPosts` function will map over all of the posts in the array, get a signed URL for the image in the post, and assign a new `imageUrl` field to the post with the signed image URL.

2. One the signed posts are returned, `SET_POSTS` is dispatched, updating the state with the posts array.

That's it; we should now be able to run the app and test it out:

```
~ npm start
```

To test out the subscription/real-time functionality, try opening a new window and running the app in both windows, viewing the posts in one window and creating a post in another window.

Summary

Here are a few things to keep in mind from this chapter:

- When working with storage, images cannot be referenced directly by their URL; they must be signed using a `Storage.get` call.

- Once a file is returned with a signed URL, it will be valid for 15 minutes by default; after that, it will expire. This can be overridden by passing in an `expires` option to set the availability of your URLs.

- When working with an array of images, you can map over the array and use `Promise.all` to get a signed URL for each item in the array.

## CHAPTER 11

Hosting: Deploying Your Application to the Amplify Console with CI and CD

Now that we've looked at building out our apps, how do we make them live and show them to the world? In this chapter, we'll look at a couple of different hosting options with Amplify, and also how to deploy your app using a custom domain name.

The service we'll be using is the Amplify Console hosting service. The Amplify Console is a fully managed hosting service that provides a simple workflow for deploying static sites and full stack serverless applications. Using Amplify Console, you deploy your code using the CLI, a GitHub repository, or manually, and the service will build and deploy your app for you.

When working with frameworks like React, Vue, Angular, or even frameworks like Gatsby, Next, or Nuxt, there is typically a *build* phase that needs to be run. This phase will take all of the JavaScript, CSS, and images and, using a module bundler such as webpack, create a deployable build of your website.

The Amplify Console will allow you to configure the app's build settings so that when you are ready to deploy a new version, the service will be able to take your raw files, then build and deploy your app to your live domain for you.

In this chapter, we'll learn about the following:

CLI-based deployments
> Using our local project, we will deploy an app to Amplify Console hosting directly from the CLI.

Git-based deployments
> Using a GitHub repository, we will deploy an app to Amplify Console hosting and learn how to trigger new builds when changes are merged into the master branch.

Access control
> Add access control to restrict access to your branches with a username and password.

Custom domains
> Use your custom domain name for the deployment.

Let's get started.

CLI-Based Deployments

In this section, we will learn how to deploy a project to Amplify Console hosting directly from the CLI.

To get started, create a new React app:

```
~ npx create-react-app fullstack-app
~ cd full-stack-app
~ npm install aws-amplify @aws-amplify/ui-react
```

Next, we'll initialize a new Amplify project and add a single service, authentication:

```
~ amplify init
# Follow the steps to give the project a name, environment name, and set the
  default text editor.
# Accept defaults for everything else and choose your AWS Profile.

~ amplify add auth
? Do you want to use the default authentication and security configuration?
  Default configuration
? How do you want users to be able to sign in? Username
? Do you want to configure advanced settings? No, I am done.
```

When running the `init` command, we are walked through the same set of questions we've been walked through in all of the previous chapters.

We are asked questions like what our source and distribution directories are, as well as the build command. By default, the Amplify CLI will detect the framework and automatically set these for you for many popular frameworks, like in our React projects.

If you are using a framework that is not recognized by the Amplify CLI, or have a custom build configuration, you may need to set these values to be something different.

To add hosting, we can use the `hosting` category:

```
~ amplify add hosting

? Select the plugin module to execute: Hosting with Amplify Console
? Choose a type: Manual Deployment
```

Next, let's update our frontend code to add a basic greeting as well as authentication.

Start by opening *src/index.js* and configuring the Amplify app by adding the following code below the last import:

```
import Amplify from 'aws-amplify'
import config from './aws-exports'
Amplify.configure(config)
```

Then update *src/App.js* with the following code:

```
import React from 'react'
import logo from './logo.svg'
import './App.css'

import { withAuthenticator } from '@aws-amplify/ui-react'

function App() {
  return (
    <div className="App">
      <header className="App-header">
        <img src={logo} className="App-logo" alt="logo" />
        <h1>Hello World!</h1>
      </header>
    </div>
  );
}

export default withAuthenticator(App, { includeGreetings: true })
```

Our app is now ready to deploy. To deploy both the frontend and backend, we can run the `publish` command. The `publish` command will deploy both the frontend *and* backend code to the Amplify Console:

```
~ amplify publish
```

Now, we should be able to view the app in the console with both the frontend deployment as well as backend service configuration:

```
~ amplify console
```

From the Amplify Console dashboard, click the app name that was just deployed. Here, you should be able to see a toggle to view both the frontend (*Frontend environments*) as well as the backend (*Backend environments*) deployments, as shown in Figure 11-1.

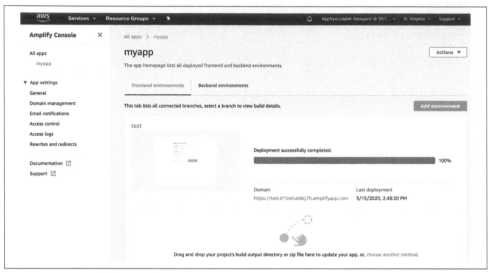

Figure 11-1. Amplify Console overview

From the *Frontend environments* view, you should be able to click the domain to view the live website hosted by the Amplify Console. The domain URL should look something like this:

```
https://env_name.deployment_id.amplifyapp.com
```

In the lefthand menu are options for things like domain management for custom domains (covered in "Custom Domains" on page 155), email notifications for build events, access control (something we will cover in this chapter), logs, and redirects.

When you make an update and need to deploy a new version, you can run the `pub lish` command again to deploy the updated version of the app.

Git-Based Deployments

Now let's look at how you can enable Git-based deployments using an Amplify app stored in a GitHub repository. While deploying from your local project works well, many times you will be working from a Git repository either alone or with a team. The Amplify Console supports Git-based hosting for your applications, along with built-in features automatic deployments on merges and feature branch deployments (branch deployments linked to each feature branch).

Let's look at how to take the app we have already built and deploy it to the Amplify Console from a GitHub repository.

The first step is to remove the existing amplify backend that we have set up:

```
~ amplify delete
```

Then, create a new Amplify app and add authentication:

```
~ amplify init
# Follow the steps to give the project a name, environment name, and set the
  default text editor.
# Accept defaults for everything else and choose your AWS Profile.

~ amplify add auth
? Do you want to use the default authentication and security configuration?
  Default configuration
? How do you want users to be able to sign in? Username
? Do you want to configure advanced settings? No, I am done.
```

Now, deploy the backend using the Amplify push command:

```
~ amplify push
```

We now need to create a GitHub repository to hold the app.

Creating the GitHub Repository

The next thing you will need to do is go to GitHub.com and create a new repository. I'll create a new repo called *my-react-app*, as shown in Figure 11-2.

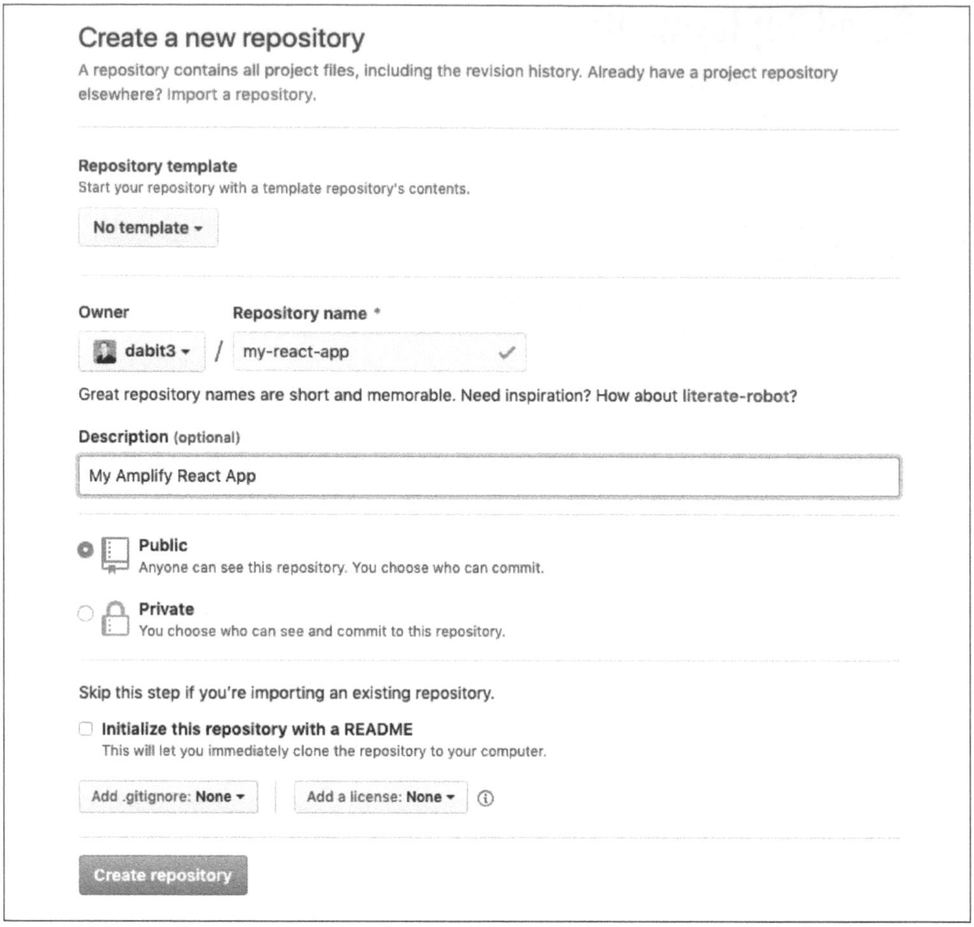

Figure 11-2. Creating a GitHub repository

Once you've created the repo, you will be given a repo URI that looks like what's shown in Figure 11-3:

```
git@github.com:dabit3/my-react-app.git
```

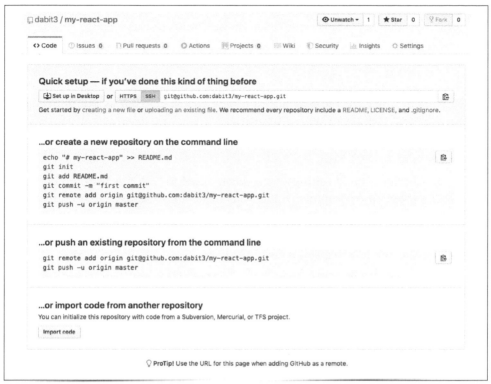

Figure 11-3. GitHub project URI

Copy this repo URI and return to the command line. From here, we will initialize a new GitHub project in our local app:

```
~ git init
~ git remote add origin git@github.com:your_github_username/my-react-app.git
```

We'll then add the files to be tracked and push the changes to our repo:

```
~ git add .
~ git commit -m 'initial commit'
~ git push origin master
```

Now that the app has been pushed to GitHub, we can connect to Amplify Console hosting. To do so, let's add it via the CLI:

```
~ amplify add hosting

? Select the plugin module to execute: Hosting with Amplify Console
? Choose a type: Continuous deployment (Git-based deployments)
```

The CLI should open the Amplify Console in your web browser, allowing you to choose GitHub as your source code provider.

1. As your first step (in the Amplify Console), choose GitHub as the source code provider and then click Connect branch.

2. Next, sign in with GitHub, then choose the new repo you just created and the master branch. Click Next.

3. In the Configure build settings page, when asked to "select a backend environment," choose the environment name you already have created.

4. Next, in the Configure build settings page, when asked to "select an existing service role or create a new one so Amplify Console may access your resources," click Create new role to create a new IAM role:

   a. Click Next: Permissions, Next: Tags, Next: Review, and then Create Role to create a new IAM role.

   b. Go back to the Configure build settings page, click the refresh button, and select the newly created role from the dropdown.

5. Click Next.

6. In the Review page, click Save and deploy to deploy the app.

The app has now been deployed to the Amplify Console and a new build will begin. When the build finishes, you should be given a live URL to view your app.

Git-Based CI/CD

Now that the app has been deployed, let's look at how to implement CD into the app.

The basic idea with Git-based CI and CD is that you can deploy and test builds to any branch by pushing directly to Git. Once the changes are merged, a new build is kicked off and a live URL is given to you to try out.

In this way, you can have feature/branch deployments, like *prod* (for production), *dev* (for development), and *feature_name* (for new features). When building in this way, you are able to test out new changes in a live environment, testing out not only the frontend but also the backend changes.

Let's try kicking off a new build. To do so, make a change to one of the local files. Update *src/App.js* with some updated text, then add the changes and push to GitHub:

```
~ git add .
~ git commit -m 'updates to App.js'
~ git push origin master
```

Now, when you open your app in the Amplify Console, you should notice a new build has been kicked off automatically for you.

Access Control

Next, let's look at how to enable access control to password protect our deployment.

Using access control, you can specify that a visitor must have a username and password to view either a deployment or a specific branch deployment. This is especially useful if you are testing out new private features that you wish to keep undiscoverable by anyone outside your team.

Here's how to enable access controls:

1. In the lefthand menu, click Access Control.
2. Next, click Manage Access.
3. Here, for the master branch, set the Access setting to Restricted, then set a username and password.

Now, open the URL for the deployment. You will notice that you will be unable to view it without entering the username and password.

In the Access Control menu, you can also choose to set access control on a branch-by-branch basis.

Custom Domains

Finally, let's learn how to use a custom domain name for our app.

To enable a custom domain, we need to do three things:

- Add the domain in Amazon Route53.
- Set the nameservers in the DNS settings of the domain provider for the domain you are using.
- Configure the Amplify Console app to use the domain added in Route 53.

Let's walk through how to do this:

1. In the Services dropdown menu in the main AWS dashboard, search for or click Route53.
2. Click Hosted Zones.
3. Click Create Hosted Zone.

4. Set the domain name by adding the URL to the Domain name input field, then click Create.

After creating the Hosted Zone, you will be given four nameserver values. You will need those values in the next step, so keep them handy. You can also navigate back to them at any time by visiting the Route53 dashboard and clicking on the domain you would like to retrieve the values for. The nameservers will look something like this:

```
ns-1020.awsdns-63.net
ns-1523.awsdns-62.org
ns-244.awsdns-30.com
ns-1724.awsdns-23.co.uk
```

1. Now, go into your hosting account (e.g., GoDaddy or Google Domains), and set these custom nameservers in your DNS setting for the domain you're using.

2. Next, back in the Amplify Console for the app for which you would like to enable a custom domain, click Domain Management in the left menu, then click the Add Domain button.

3. Here, the drop-down menu should show you the domain you have in Route53. Choose this domain and click Configure domain.

This should deploy the app to your custom domain (it will take 5–30 minutes for the DNS to propagate).

Summary

Here are a few things to keep in mind from this chapter:

- The Amplify Console hosts both backend and as well as frontend deployments.
- There are two main ways to deploy the frontend to the Amplify Console, from your local project or from a Git repository. You can also upload projects manually or host them from Dropbox.
- Once your app is hosted, you can then set up things like password protection, custom domains, and branch deployments by configuring your deployment in the Amplify Console.

Index

Symbols

A

Axios library, installing, 27

B

BaaS (backend as a service), 2
backend, 114-117, 150
backend folder, 14
bucket testing, 4
business logic, 2, 4, 65
business value, 2, 3
Button component, 66

C

calling APIs, 26
canPerformAction function, 97
catch block, 43
checkUser function, 101
checkUser.js file, 100
CI/CD (continuous integration and continuous deployment), 147-156
CLI-based deployments, 148
client app
    configuring, 25
    updating, 29
client authentication, 54
client library, 6, 21
client-side code, writing, 132, 140
"Cloud Programming Simplified: A Berkeley View on Serverless Computing", 2
cloud computing, growth of, 16
Cloudflare Workers, 7
CloudFormation, 6, 8
code
    as a benefit of serverless architecture, 5
    client-side, 132, 140
Cognito
    about, 1, 52-53
    event data, 82
    how it works, 52
    integrating with AWS Amplify, 53
    user pools authentication type, 112
Cognito groups, 101, 112
Cognito identity pools, 112
Cognito user pool, 52, 83, 112, 123
CoinLore API, 27
coins route, creating, 23
complex object storage, 7, 9
components, creating, 56
configure command, 11
configuring

AmplifyCLI, 11
API Gateway endpoint, 30
applications, 62
client app, 25
triggers, 83
ConfirmSignUp component, 69
confirmSignUp function, 69, 71
conflict detection, 128
Container component, 56, 101, 118
Container.js file, 55, 100
cost, as a benefit of serverless architecture, 3
creating
    Amplify app, 113
    APIs, 19, 24, 30, 139
    applications, 55-62
    AppSync GraphQL API, 131, 139
    backend, 114-117
    base projects, 83, 131, 139
    coins route, 23
    components, 56
    custom authentication forms, 65-77
    file/folder structure, 55
    frontend, 100-107, 117-126
    GitHub repository, 151
    GraphQL API, 34
    Lambda functions, 30
    notes, 42
    offline apps with Amplify DataStore, 130-135
    protectedRoute hook, 63
    React application, 21, 38-49, 53
    real-time apps with Amplify DataStore, 130-135
    reducers, 40
    serverless functions, 20-23
CRUD+L (create, read, update, delete, and list), 31
cryptofunction folder/function, 22
CSS, 61
#current-cloud-backend folders, 14
custom authentication forms
    about, 65
    completing, 71
    ConfirmSignUp component, 69
    creating, 65-77
    ForgotPassword component, 70
    ForgotPasswordSubmit component, 70
    form type toggles, 75
    renderForm function, 73

localStorage, 9

M

Main component, 106
Main.js file, 100
managed services, 3
Menu component, 57
MFA (multifactor authentication), 51, 69
microservice architecture, 9
Microsoft Azure, 5
models, importing, 128
mutations (writes/updates), 10

N

nameservers, 155
native Android, 9
native iOS, 9
Nav component, 57, 102, 119
Nav.js file, 55, 100
Netlify Functions, 7
Next, 147
Node Version Manager, 11
Node.js, 5, 11
notes
    creating, 42
    deleting, 45
    listing, 38-41
    updating, 46
Nuxt, 147

O

OAUTH (open authentication), 51
observe operation, 131
offline apps, building (see Amplify DataStore)
offline functionality, testing, 135
Okta, 51
onCreateNote event, 49
OpenID Connect authentication type, 112
operational responsibilities, 3
operations
    Amplify DataStore, 128
    GraphQL, 33
optimistic concurrency conflict-resolution
    strategy, 128
optimistic response, 43
over-fetching, 31

P

pass in, 28, 60, 77, 97, 116, 126
path argument, 25
Performance component, 121
Performance route, 121
Performance type, 110
permissions, IAM (Identity and Access Man-
    agement), 83
persist, 9, 52
post method, 80, 96, 98, 106
predicates, Amplify DataStore, 129
primary key, 94, 110
private files, 137
Profile component, 60, 72, 76, 103
profile data, displaying, 61
profile route, 51
Profile.js file, 55, 100
projects
    creating base, 83, 131, 139
    initializing, 12
promise, 26, 27
Protected component, 58
protected files, 138
protected routes, 51, 63
Protected.js file, 55
protectedRoute hook, 63
Public component, 56
public files, 137
public route, 51
Public.js file, 55
publish command, 149
push command, 24, 28, 36, 54
put method, 80, 96, 106

Q

queries (reads), 10
query operation, 130
queryStringParameters property, 28

R

re-render, 72, 77
React application
    creating, 21, 38-49, 53
    rendering data in, 26
    uploading images from, 88
React Color, 131
React Context, 1
React Native, 53

About the Author

Nader Dabit is a web and mobile developer who specializes in building cross-platform and cloud-enabled applications. At Amazon Web Services, he works with the client teams to help develop features and improve developer experience for client-side SDKs. Prior to working with AWS, Nader trained companies like Microsoft, Amazon, Salesforce, and American Express on how to build applications using the React and React Native frameworks through his company, React Native Training.

Colophon

The animal on the cover of *Full Stack Serverless* is a blue tang (*Paracanthurus hepatus*). These fish are found across a large area of the Indian and Pacific oceans. Blue tang have many other common names, such as doctorfish, palette surgeonfish, flagtail surgeonfish, and hippo tang.

Adult blue tangs have oval-shaped bodies and vivid blue coloring, with darker blue stripes running along the dorsal area from eye to tail. They also have bright yellow pectoral and caudal fins. Juveniles are yellow with blue spots around their eyes. Blue tangs average 8 to 12 inches long as adults, and weigh just over 1 pound. Their lifespan in the wild is 8 to 12 years.

Blue tangs live on coral reefs or in rocky areas where there is a large amount of algae, the main item in their diet. They provide a valuable service to the reef ecosystem by removing excess algae and preventing the coral from suffocating. Their sharp teeth and the small shape of their mouth allows them to feed from uneven surfaces.

Blue tangs usually live in schools made up of various species of fish, which provides protection and helps secure food sources. They are known for playing dead when they encounter predators. In addition, the blue tang has sharp spines along the top and bottom of its body and an extensible envenomed spine in its tail fin that can produce deep, painful wounds in predators such as tuna and grouper. Males also use these spines in "sword fights" to establish dominance.

This species is popular in aquariums—in part because the popular character Dory from the Pixar/Disney films *Finding Nemo* (2003) and *Finding Dory* (2016) is a blue tang. Many of the animals on O'Reilly covers are endangered; all of them are important to the world.

The color cover illustration is by Susan Thompson, based on a black-and-white image found in *Natural History: Fishes* (1849) by Philip Henry Gosse. The cover fonts are Gilroy Semibold and Guardian Sans. The text font is Adobe Minion Pro; the heading font is Adobe Myriad Condensed; and the code font is Dalton Maag's Ubuntu Mono.

O'REILLY®

There's much more
where this came from.

Experience books, videos, live online
training courses, and more from O'Reilly
and our 200+ partners—all in one place.

Learn more at oreilly.com/online-learning

9 781492 059899